Concern for Church Renewal

CONCERN for Church Renewal

Essays on Community and Discipleship,
1958–1966

CONCERN: A Pamphlet Series for
Questions of Christian Renewal

EDITED BY
Laura Schmidt Roberts

WIPF & STOCK · Eugene, Oregon

CONCERN FOR CHURCH RENEWAL
Essays on Community and Discipleship, 1958–1966

CONCERN: A Pamphlet Series for Questions of Christian Renewal

Copyright © 2022 Wipf and Stock Publishers. All rights reserved. Except for brief quotations in critical publications or reviews, no part of this book may be reproduced in any manner without prior written permission from the publisher. Write: Permissions, Wipf and Stock Publishers, 199 W. 8th Ave., Suite 3, Eugene, OR 97401.

Wipf & Stock
An Imprint of Wipf and Stock Publishers
199 W. 8th Ave., Suite 3
Eugene, OR 97401

www.wipfandstock.com

PAPERBACK ISBN: 978-1-7252-6098-6
HARDCOVER ISBN: 978-1-7252-6099-3
EBOOK ISBN: 978-1-7252-6100-6

03/09/22

Contents

Series Foreword | vii
Introduction by Laura Schmidt Roberts | xi

Historical Essays

1. Marginalia (excerpt, 1960) | 3
   JOHN HOWARD YODER

2. Marginalia (excerpt, 1958) | 7
   JOHN HOWARD YODER

3. The Church in the House | 9
   HANS-RUEDI WEBER

4. The House Church in the New Testament | 27
   QUINTUS LEATHERMAN

5. Can the Adult Sunday School Class be the "House" within Which the True Church Is Experienced? | 31
   PAUL M. MILLER

6. Group Dynamics in Evangelism (by Paul Miller): A Review Article | 40
   ALBERT STEINER

7. Evangelism Through the Dynamics of a Christian Group | 43
   GERALD C. STUDER

CONTENTS

8   Small Congregations | 51
    VIRGIL VOGT

9   Changing Forms of the Church and Her Witness | 64
    LELAND HARDER

10 The Renewal of the Church | 94
    JOHN W. MILLER

11 Marginalia: A Syllabus of Issues | 113
    JOHN HOWARD YODER

12 The Order that Belongs to the Gospel | 120
    LEWIS BENSON

Contemporary Responses

13 After Yoder: Failure, Authenticity, and the Renewal
    of the Mennonite Church | 135
    SUSANNE GUENTHER LOEWEN

14 A Global Communion as a Condition for the Possibility
    of Church Renewal | 148
    CÉSAR GARCÍA

    Appendix: Listing of all *CONCERN* republication volumes | 157
    Bibliography | 165

Series Foreword to the 2022 Edition

In 1952 a group of seven young American Mennonite intellectuals studying in Europe convened for a two-week theological retreat in Amsterdam to discuss the place of Mennonites in what they saw as the modern, "post-Christendom" world. Most all had come to post-war Europe with Canadian or American Mennonite organizations to assist mission, relief, and rebuilding efforts. They are, in the words of one participant, overwhelmed by what they encounter—the theology, imagery, procedures, and practices they bring are inadequate to their work and witness in postwar Europe. They have many questions about what it means to be the church—to be disciples—in that time and place; questions compounded by conversations and studies that open up for them the ideological and philosophical currents sweeping Europe at the time.

What becomes clear in the papers presented in Amsterdam and the subsequently published series *Concern: A Pamphlet Series for Questions of Christian Renewal* (1954–71) is a common concern over a gap between an Anabaptist vision and contemporary Mennonite reality.[1] They view the increasingly hierarchical denominational structure of the Mennonite church in Canada and the United States and its institution-building as inconsistent with an Anabaptist notion of church as community. These structural forms and the accompanying concerns for their perpetuation reflect "Protestantizing" compromise instead of Anabaptist movement-oriented, mission-minded, evangelical zeal. The writers instead call for a more radical and authentic expression of the Christian life. They call for a renewal that would

---

1. Toews, *Mennonites in American Society*, 232. For more on the historical genesis of *Concern* see the front pieces of Vogt, *Roots of CONCERN*, and Hershberger, "Power, Tradition, and Renewal."

realign the mission, leadership, and organization of the church as well as its relationship to broader society in ways more resonant with the tenets of a culturally-engaged Anabaptism; which is to say, they call for a Mennonite response to modernity which is both faithful to their construal of Anabaptist tradition and appropriate to the times.[2]

While *Concern: A Pamphlet Series for Questions of Christian Renewal* and the movement it inspired address the context of the day, the call issued to discern what it means to be a faithful church in and for the times—ever the church's call—is one we face with growing urgency in today's postmodern context. What theology, imagery, and practices are adequate to the work and witness of disciples in this time and place? What is church *for*? Republishing these essays makes more readily available for this task resources shaped by Anabaptist tradition. The themes and issues the essays raise remain relevant: Christian responsibility in and to the "world," the goal of history, critical engagement with political ideologies and economic theories, global mission and the colonial legacy of Christendom, the unavoidably enculturated nature of lived faith, the gifts of the Spirit, desire for renewed (radicalized?) authentic expressions of faith, Anabaptist-shaped church structure and pastoral leadership, the fraught realities of communal authority and discipline.

But the model the pamphlet series provides is equally important. Especially at its inception, *Concern* was intended to be a forum for works in progress versus polished churchly or academic pieces—a place to test ideas, raise questions, challenge practices, even change one's mind. The pamphlets present articles reflecting varying viewpoints intended to promote discussion, critical reflection, and ultimately transformation of understanding, practices, and structured forms of Christian discipleship. This example of dialog across difference as a shared path toward renewal is welcome in the current increasingly polarized context, where disagreement seems more likely to end a conversation than begin one.

Response essays from contemporary Mennonite writers in each volume continue in this vein, critically engaging the contribution and limitations of the historical essays and building out concerns of their own in the current global, ecclesial, and historical climate. One aspect of that climate is especially important to state clearly: the mixed legacy of *Concern* writer

---

2. See Vogt, "Foreword," in *The Roots of CONCERN*. Sawatsky, "Editorial," iii. *The Conrad Grebel Review* 8.2 contains articles on and reflections by participants in the *Concern* movement.

and sometime editor, theologian and ethicist John Howard Yoder, whose sexual abuse must be acknowledged.[3] The depth and breadth of harm Yoder perpetrated, most horrifically on those he abused, and also on the shape and substance of Anabaptist-Mennonite theology and ecclesiology, is difficult to fathom. While significant deconstruction of Yoder's work has been done, grappling with the aftermath and implications continues.[4] Refusing to engage or promote Yoder's work as a whole or selectively is one avenue of response. Such selectivity is evident in this series; most, but not all, of Yoder's essays have been republished here. Some material already widely available, and especially the content or use of which harmed victim-survivors of Yoder's abuse, has not been included. Another avenue of response takes encounters with his thought (in church, in institutions, in print) as an occasion to reframe discussion of it: by first speaking the truth of his serial sexual abuse and then reconsidering his work in light of that context. This series also does some of that work selectively, at the choice of several contemporary response writers and in this acknowledgment prefacing each volume. *Concern* should not be reduced to Yoder's contributions. While persistent, Yoder's voice is but one among many across the original pamphlets. On their own, the other fifty-plus writers give rich, contextualized, and diverse expression to theological, ecclesiological, and missiological explorations in the mid-twentieth century.

A historical republication project such as this is not possible without the expert help of librarians and archivists. I owe such debts in too many places to name but the greatest—to Fresno Pacific University's Hiebert Library Director Kevin Enns-Rempel, archivist Hannah Keeney, and research librarian David Hasegawa—must be mentioned. I have benefitted from the university's support through a sabbatical leave dedicated to this project, multiple Provost's Faculty Research Grants, and the Fresno Pacific Biblical Seminary's Center for Anabaptist Studies donation toward publication costs. I greatly appreciate other contributions toward those costs from the Schafer-Friesen Research Fund (Goshen College), the Gerhard Lohrenz

---

3. See Waltner Goossen, "'Defanging the Beast.'" Waltner Goossen catalogs both Yoder's serial sexual abuse and institutional failure to respond adequately to his victims or Yoder himself.

4. In addition to the many articles in *Mennonite Quarterly Review* 89.1, see for example Anabaptist Mennonite Biblical Seminary, "AMBS Response to Victims"; Cramer et al., "Theology and Misconduct"; "On Teaching John Howard Yoder" collection of essays by Mennonite faculty from various institutions in *Mennonite Life* 68 (2014); Soto Albrecht and Stephens, eds. *Liberating the Politics of Jesus*.

SERIES FOREWORD TO THE 2022 EDITION

Publication Fund (Canadian Mennonite University), and the Conrad Grebel University College Theological Studies Program. I am especially grateful to the Mennonite Faith and Learning Society (British Columbia), whose work first became known to me through its sponsorship of the Humanitas Anabaptist Centre (Trinity Western University), and whose very generous support of this publication shows concretely their stated commitment to advance education and scholarship from an Anabaptist perspective.

Thanks are due to Fresno Pacific colleagues in the Division of Biblical and Religious Studies, especially Quentin Kinnison, to Rod Janzen, and to Larry Dunn, for unflagging support, probing questions, and insightful feedback along the way. This project would not have come to me without Ched Myers' suggestion and encouragement, and would not have come to completion without the steadfast guidance and input of Ted Lewis at Wipf and Stock. Thank you both for the gift of this work. Finally, I am deeply grateful to the contemporary response writers in each volume of the series whose essays model so well what Paul Ricoeur would call a "refiguring" of tradition. Thank you for grappling with the plurality and ambiguity of tradition in ways that challenge and potentially revitalize it through theology and praxis from and for actual current ecclesial communities, Anabaptist and otherwise.

An appendix in each book in this series lists the contents of the seven total volumes comprising the *Concern* republication project initiated under the editorial direction of Virgil Vogt which this series completes.[5]

Laura Schmidt Roberts
Fresno Pacific University
September 2021

---

5. In addition to this four-volume, thematically organized series, three other volumes complete the Wipf and Stock republication of the *Concern* pamphlets: Vogt, *Roots of CONCERN* and *CONCERN for Education*; Vogt and Roberts, *Concern for Anabaptist Renewal*.

Introduction

From its first volume in 1954, *Concern* ran statements identifying it as an *independent* pamphlet series focused on Christian renewal, the contents of which were neither definitive or agreed upon by everyone in the editorial group due to its purpose: to stimulate study and discussion.[1] This volume gathers together essays wrestling with questions of what approaches or formats might "structure" church renewal. Editorial comments from the original *Concern* 12 indicate the intentional juxtaposition of views on these themes, and both there and in *Concern* 5 further contributions to expand the discussion are invited. Writers address matters of renewal in reference to a Believers' Church or Anabaptist framework, reflecting differing viewpoints but a shared sense that community and discipleship are essential. The essays document the shape of this debate among mid twentieth-century Mennonites in Canada and the United States, providing a unique resource for Anabaptists (and others) addressing similar concerns today.

The volume begins with a brief excerpt by John Howard Yoder[2] identifying *Concern* as a child of the "rediscovery of the Anabaptist Vision" in its pursuit of relevant ecclesial reform informed by an array of historical and biblical sources. Following this broad framing, essays from the original *Concern* 5 (1958) present a range of views on the house church as a path to Christian renewal. They wrestle with what constitutes a church,

---

1. For the origins and context of *Concern: A Pamphlet Series for Questions of Christian Renewal* (1954–71) please see the Series Foreword to this volume.

2. This volume contains work by John Howard Yoder, whose sexual abuse is a well-established fact which must be acknowledged. Please see the Foreword for more about the editor's choice to republish Yoder's work in this series.

whether existing structures can engender renewal, and assert that, however organized, the church must be planted in the *oikos*—"where life concerns converge." New Testament and house church models scaffold discussion of communities of discipleship as central to the true church and its desired renewal.

Similarly, editorial comments ("Marginalia") from the original *Concern* 12 (1966) provide a study guide intended to facilitate comparison and discussion across the lengthy church renewal-focused essays by Leland Harder and John W. Miller. Though with markedly different approach, each in the end identifies communities of discipleship based on New Testament models as the path to renewal, as did the house church articles. The historical essays conclude with a piece by Quaker author Lewis Benson which both resonates with and challenges the preceding writings. Benson identifies the path for Christian renewal not as restoration of the pattern of the New Testament church (the view he attributes to Anabaptism) but as "becoming related to Christ in a master-disciple relationship and finding through this relationship fellowship with one another."

The volume closes with response essays by two contemporary authors who critically engage the historical writings as they consider the shape of renewal needed by church communities today. Susanne Guenther Loewen observes the failure of the Mennonite Church to respond to sexual abuse as a serious and pervasive peace issue and the loss of authentic community which results. She asserts that the path of renewal lies in facing and owning this failure, for only then can integrity and authenticity as a community embodying a holistic justice and peace be recovered. César García argues that a global communion (an organic, relational "Anabaptist catholicity") provides the possibility of renewal by fostering unity, interdependency, and a transnational, Christ-centered identity in which structural economic inequalities and racial systems of domination may be overcome. He explores what might "structure" the realization of such a vision. Their work demonstrates the persistent need for church renewal and the importance, now as when the historical writings were new, of pursuing that call in the messy realites of actual, concrete, communal life.

Historical Essays

1

Marginalia (excerpt, 1960)

JOHN HOWARD YODER

No mention has been made in the pages of *Concern* of the publication nearly three years ago of the symposium *The Recovery of the Anabaptist Vision*.[1] *Concern* is not interested in joining the ranks of book-reviewing periodicals, and yet the relation of this volume to problems of Christian renewal demands that its appearance be noted, and its significance weighed. The idea of a volume bringing together the fruits of a quarter century of Anabaptist scholarship and at the same time giving recognition to the contribution of H. S. Bender to this field of study was proposed early in 1955. What was then projected as a special number of *Concern* grew into a significant book, for which, fortunately, more adequate editorial leadership and publishing sponsorship were found than *Concern* could have provided. The book has received very friendly reviews and in two years has sold over one thousand copies, a quite respectable figure for a work of its type.

The book calls for notice primarily as a major milestone in the rehabilitation of the sixteenth-century free churches by Protestant theological thought. The very first serious historical studies treating Anabaptism in an objective, scholarly way appeared just a century ago. But only in the last thirty years has the new historical material been unearthed in sufficient quantity and interpreted in sufficient clarity to gain the attention of thinkers beyond the ranks of Reformation specialists and to precipitate a revision not only of historical commonplaces but even of theological

1. Hershberger, *Recovery*.

assumptions. It is no longer possible intelligently to speak of the Reformation and of occidental church history since then without dealing with the major church type which was reborn in the midst of fear and trembling in a clandestine prayer meeting a few steps up the alley from Zürich's Grossmünster, one January night in 1525.

But what matters is not that a long-standing wrong of official historiography is being righted. Far more significant than this is the fact that the conception of the church and of the Christian life whose exemplification in Anabaptism is being rediscovered is today of extraordinary relevance. This is true firstly because the Reformation's attempt to maintain a "Constantinian" pattern of responsibility for society is being recognized to have been both pragmatically and theologically dubious, and European thinkers within the *Volkskirche* tradition are denouncing it, raising the question whether there is an alternative more consonant with the gospel. Secondly, the rediscovery of Anabaptism is significant because it coincides with a mighty surge of interest in the doctrine of the church, stimulated by a new current in Biblical theology, by a revived awareness of the missionary task, and by the ecumenical movement. The Anabaptist rejection of the concept of "Christendom" is now followed by men like Lesslie Newbigin,[2] even though their churches are historically unexplainable apart from mass-church assumptions.

Thirdly, the rediscovery of the Anabaptist vision is crucially important for that small segment of the church which stands in the Anabaptist-Mennonite tradition and faces the staggering task of redefining its stance of faith in modern terms, deciding whether and how to deny that the only choice is between a culturally buttressed isolation and a conformity to prevailing culture rendered less distasteful by a slogan like "responsibility."

Seen from these three viewpoints, it is providential that a fresh understanding of the Anabaptist example should have been won just now. *Concern* is in a real sense a child of this rediscovery; *Concern* No. 1 can best be understood as a testimony to the discovery that the "Anabaptist Vision," both as a Christian goal and as a regulative concept in Christian thought, was more true, more basic, and more crucial than we had previously realized.

But is it right for Christians to give this much attention to one narrow slice of church history? Is it not out of place in the "ecumenical age" to give renewed attention to a small group's peculiar heritage? Could not the

2. See for example the introduction to Newbigin, *Household*.

study of the New Testament and of the needs of our day lead committed Christians to discover the fullness of God's will for them without their borrowing a crutch from the sixteenth century? This is a very reasonable objection. If Christian faith were a system of disincarnate generalities, it would in fact be an invincible argument. Yet to point to it to disqualify the study of the lessons of church history would be to deny that we are already involved, not only by error but also by virtue of the gospel, in the triumphs and treasons of the church across the ages.

The fundamental problem which faces the advocates of church renewal is a question with which neither Bible study nor the analysis of the present scene will suffice to answer. For the question is not what the Bible teaches, but whether this teaching can be applied in another age than that of the Bible; not whether the Christian faith must be expressed in forms relevant to contemporary man, but whether in order to do this the original faith itself must be modified. The answer of most church leaders since the fourth century and of most influential thinkers today is that there exists so fundamental an incompatibility between the message of the New Testament, calling out a pilgrim people to follow their Master in warfare against this present age, and on the other hand the dictate of the contemporary situation, demanding total involvement in society, that certain basic aspects of the New Testament view of the church and the world must be abandoned or thoroughly redefined. This was the view of the Protestant Reformers, as it is today that of most Protestant teachers. Here, and not on the level of Biblical interpretation, is the crucial issue. This is the question to which neither the New Testament nor the modern scene speaks, for it asks how the two are related. Here it is that the Anabaptists were both original and clear. The position they took was clearer, just at this point, as far as present scholarship knows, than that of any other major movement of renewal within Christendom. Their testimony was, as ours must be, that the New Testament view of the church is in its core just as final, just as authoritative, just as adequate for other ages, as the New Testament doctrine of justification by faith. They maintained this view in a context where the refrain, "times have changed," was just as believable as today. For this reason, they merit our attention in a special way.

Any direct transposition of particular Anabaptist patterns to our age would involve misunderstanding the sense in which the Anabaptist example is valid for us. Such an enterprise is further excluded by the lack of formal unity of the various Anabaptist groups, although their diversities tend to be overemphasized by contemporary scholars. But the missionary passion, the radical discipleship, and the views of the Bible and of the church, which stood behind both of these, were common to all three major segments of sixteenth-century Anabaptism and remain a live option today. History, both that of Anabaptism insofar as it held to this position, and that of Protestantism, insofar as it remained consistent with its rejection thereof, confirms what the Anabaptists knew by faith: there is no other foundation.

2

Marginalia (excerpt, 1958)

JOHN HOWARD YODER

It may not be superfluous, at a moment when the return of two members of the sponsoring group of *Concern* from the academic world to more exposed outposts of witness and service has made necessary a shifting of editorial responsibilities, to restate the thinking behind the publishing of one more pamphlet series in a world abundantly provided with reading matter. This restatement may well take the form of an answer to the frequent question, "Why could not the material used in *Concern* find its way into existing Christian periodicals?" This question is not profound, nor is it logically the first one to ask, but answering it will suffice for the present as an approach to the formulation of a reason for existing.

Concern intends to publish writings which should not appear elsewhere because they are not fully "ripe." A normal Christian periodical, especially a denominational organ, is responsible to edify its readers, in the best sense of that term; this means that some kinds of wrestling with problems not yet resolved, and seeking to understand phenomena not yet fully grasped, are not in their rightful place in such a publication. Such wrestling and seeking must be done, and there are good reasons for their being shared in writing with Christian brethren, but until some conclusion is reached, they are not ready for propagation. Every issue of *Concern* thus far has therefore carried the statement that "since articles are published for the sake of study and discussion, they do not purport to be definitive." *Concern*'s sponsoring circle has had and continues to have certain preoccupations and convictions in common; but the publication itself means to further discussion, not to propagate a once-for-all fixed "platform." Dissenting contributions are solicited, and we sincerely regret that a cumulation of delays and negligences prevented one such contribution (taking issue with the material in *Concern* No. 1) from being used before the writer found occasion to make it available through other channels.

Secondly, *Concern* publishes material which is at once too long and involved for a denominational organ, and insufficiently academic for scholarly publications. Not every kind of long text, especially if it is a "seeking," undefinitive expression, lends itself to serial presentation, nor should a denominational weekly burden itself often with serial material. Those more scholarly publications which do use longer articles rightly demand a degree of academic and literary quality—and of abstraction—which cannot be required in the conversation for which *Concern* seeks to be a channel.

Thirdly, *Concern* intends to publish material of interest to readers who are not all served by any one denominational organ. It might even be found wise—this is a point at which our readers' counsel is solicited—for *Concern* to reprint from such periodicals certain articles which would normally not come to the attention of readers outside of the particular branch that journal serves.

A brief examination of annual indexes demonstrates abundantly that the sponsors and writers of *Concern* do their full share of writing for their church periodicals. Their writing at the same time in *Concern* is an evidence not of any divisive intent but rather of their reluctance to submit for publication in a context of instruction and edification thoughts which as yet are ready only for discussion. It may be hoped that the enlargement of the sponsoring group which has begun with this number (see the inside front cover) will serve to broaden the base for this necessary dialogue, and that further voices of corroboration, correction, and dissent will make themselves heard.

3

The Church in the House[1]

Hans-Ruedi Weber

One of the most impressive worship services I ever attended was in a very poor house of a working-class family south of Rome. A Protestant family had come from Sicily to that small industrial town. When the father died, the family asked for a Protestant funeral. As there was no Protestant minister in that area, a professor of theology from the Waldensian faculty in Rome came down, and to his surprise he found all the fellow workers of the Protestant who had died at the funeral. All were members of the Communist Party and, although nominal members of the Roman Catholic Church, had long since lost all contact with that church.

It was at that funeral that for the first time they heard the glad tidings of the gospel. They were so touched, that they asked the professor to come down again and again to tell them more. They met in the hall of the Communist Party and listened eagerly to the message of the Bible. There were heated debates, but also many pastoral conversations. Quite spontaneously a Protestant community was growing up in the town and its rural environment.

The (Protestant) church was there, although they had no church buildings yet nor a full-time minister. The church was growing spiritually as they held regular worship services, studied the Bible, and began to have daily family prayers. The church grew outwardly, as quite spontaneously the workers and farmers became witnesses in their work and leisure time.

1. Condensed from Weber, "Church in the House," *Laity*.

When I visited these worshiping, serving, and witnessing communities, a Protestant minister had just begun to work among them. But they still had no church buildings. So we met in the dining room of one of those bare houses the workers had built themselves in their spare time through mutual aid. And somehow the spirit of mutuality characterized the whole service. We used an austere Reformed liturgy—which suddenly came alive and was what it is meant to be: the drama of God meeting man through his presence in law, forgiveness, and new direction, through word and sacrament. The sermon was not a monologue as it was interrupted by spontaneous questions and exclamations. The holy communion brought together—as it is meant to do—the sacred and the secular, the holy and the common. The bread and the wine were the same as we ate and drank later at lunch. The communion table was the homemade table, where the family who lived in the house assembled for every meal. Even the gestures of "breaking the bread" and "pouring out the wine" were the same familiar gestures you see during the meals in these Italian working-class families. Everything was so familiar and common during that holy communion, and yet "it came to pass, as he sat at meat with them, he took bread, and blessed it, and brake, and gave to them. And their eyes were opened, and they knew him" (Luke 24:30–31).

After that service the congregation took me to the place where they were going to build their church. Already the foundation was laid. Many church members still lived with their families in one- or two-room slum apartments; yet they gave their free time and spare money to build the "house of God."

It was good to see their eager joy and pride in that building project. And yet, when I saw the foundation of the planned church building I could not resist a feeling of sadness: Will this spontaneous Christian community soon be another mediocre Protestant congregation, where an unbridgeable gulf separates the "house of God" from the houses of the different families, the sacred from the secular, the holy from the common, faith from work? Will that church building accelerate the tendency to replace spontaneity by institutionalism and organization? Will the dialogical proclamation degenerate into monological declamation? And will the laity (the members of the people of God), now on Sundays and weekdays a worshiping, ministering and witnessing community, soon become an aloof church public, which appears only on Sundays to sit and listen?

That feeling of sadness does not merely reveal a romantic nostalgia which idealizes the New Testament church and the churches of the first generation all over the world and all through church history. It springs far more from the conviction that we paralyze the life and work of the people of God if we see the "house church" only as a temporary expedient, a provisional structure characteristic of the earliest church in Jerusalem or any other mission area, which serves only until the parish church or local congregation with its church building can be constituted. In the following we will (I) define more clearly what we mean by "house churches," and (II) explain how the constituent elements of the church are shown in the house church. We will then (III) examine the significance of the house church for the mission, unity and renewal of the church, and finally (IV) we shall ask to what extent the house church throws a new light on the respective ministries of pastor and laity.

I. The House Church: Something New?

What do we mean with the term "house church"? Is it a real "church"? And what sort of "house" have we to visualize? These are the questions to be answered in this first chapter.

The Church of God at Home

It is significant to note that in the New Testament the same term, *ekklesia*, is used to designate (i) the universal church, (ii) the church of God in a certain province or region, (iii) a particular local church, and (iv) the actual assembly of believers in any place, for instance in the upper room of a home. It is not only the addition of many local expressions of the church which makes the church; but in every gathering in the name of Christ, even in the smallest one of two or three persons, the whole church appears. This is so because the church receives its essence exclusively from God—Father, Son, and Holy Spirit. In all the (over eighty) terms and images employed by New Testament writers to designate the church, God (and very especially the person and work of Christ) is assumed to be central and determinative for its life. This all-decisive Person is not bound by numbers. He can turn a handful of men and women, just as easily as millions of people, into a true church.

An equally noteworthy element is the fact that in the whole New Testament the word "church" is never used to describe a building. It always describes a people or a body. Even where the term "building" is used to describe the church, it is used as an image: "like living stones, be yourselves built into a spiritual house, to be a holy priesthood . . . God's own people" (1 Pet 2:4, 9).

Much of the present-day rank-and-file thinking about the church, however, is almost exclusively church-building-centered. How many pastors, laymen, and laywomen conceive "church work" only in terms of work done on church premises or under church organizations! Our terminology betrays us: We speak of "going to church," our traditional evangelism is an invitation "to come to church," and in our common understanding "church workers" are those whose work is especially linked with the church building or church institution. Even the use of the term "laity" (derived from *laos*, which means "people," the people of God) has been affected by this church-building-centered thinking: too often a "good, active layman" is understood to mean nothing else than a man or woman who spends much time, money, and energy in and on church buildings and church organizations. How timely was the warning voiced in the preparatory survey for the sixth section at Evanston: "The organized Christian community, as represented by pastors, elders or council, must stop measuring the faithfulness toward the church, and indeed the Christian faith of laymen, by the hours they spend on church premises or in religious organizations. In most cases, the vocation of the layman as a living member of the church does not lie in the church building, the parish hall or the vestry, but rather in his office or workshop, in the working community or occupational organization, in his family and in his participation in the life of the nation and its smaller communities."

Congregations which have lost their church buildings through the hazards of war and churches in totalitarian countries which had to abandon all their organizations and institutions, suddenly discovered that they continue to be the church even without any buildings and organizations. Indeed, it requires much imagination for us to realize that the early church had no buildings but met in the homes of its members. These gatherings were called "house churches"—*he kat' oikon ekklesia*.[2]

"I believe that the theological recovery of this notion of the church in the house . . . is one of the most important tasks of our generation. Whereas

---

2. Rom 16:5; 1 Cor 16:19; Col 4:15; Phlm 2.

the organization is an optional extra . . . I believe that the cellular structure of the church will be rediscovered as a necessity of its life." When Dr. John A. T. Robinson wrote these sentences in a challenging article on "The House Church and the Parish Church"[3] he did not know that in his own country his postulates were being implemented by Canon E. W. Southcott and his congregation in the parish of Halton, Leeds. And Halton is by no means the only place where experiments are made in this direction.

Similar developments are happening in some congregations of the Church of Scotland and the Highams Park Baptist Church, London. All the churches and movements which are at present re-establishing the work of small groups, fellowships, cells, or whatever they may be called, have at least rediscovered part of the truth which is being discovered now in the Anglican parish of Halton. The different *îlots de quartiers* of France and Switzerland, the *Hausbibelkreise* and the *Hauskreise* of some evangelical academies and of the former members of the *Studentengemeinden* in Germany could be mentioned. Similar Bible study and discussion groups are widely developing in other European countries, especially in Holland and Norway. The "fellowship groups" of the Church of the Saviour in Washington, DC, are another striking example. Many denominational and interdenominational movements and fraternities like "Toc H," Christian cell movements, the "Servants of Christ the King," and the "Yokefellows" could be mentioned. Also, many recent developments in the Roman Catholic Church and much of the work done through the different lay movements in the Orthodox Church in Greece point in the same direction. Finally, a great number of instances could be found in the recent history of missions.

No up-to-date survey exists of all such attempts to build up a real fellowship within the church. But worldwide studies, like the one on "the place and use of the Bible in the church" at present being undertaken jointly by the United Bible Societies and the World Council of Churches, reveal the astonishing spread and variety of such living Christian community groups as well as their crucial importance for the life and mission of the church.

The common factor of these many developments is the assertion that a cellular structure is essential for the church. The church must be a honeycomb of small units. A diocese, synod-district, or any other regional manifestation of the church is not an agglomeration of individuals or a federation of church organizations (women's guilds, men's clubs, youth groups, missionary circles, etc.); it is rather an organic union of parishes or

---

3. Robinson, "House Church and the Parish."

local congregations. But also, the parish or local congregation is not just a collection of Christian individuals or local church organizations. It should be a honeycomb of many miniature manifestations of the whole church, i.e., units which are not exclusively sectional groupings founded on some specific and limited basis of sex, age, or interest. The house church should essentially be of the same substance as the lump.

This conception of the cellular structure of the church was very strong in early Christian times: The church lived and spread "by houses." The same conception was the reason for John Wesley's insistence that every Methodist must be a member of a class meeting. But already during the first Christian centuries and after the establishment of the almost exclusively parochial structure of the church the significance of such "house churches" has been grievously lost in most of the Christian churches.

If the house church is "church" in the full sense of this word, all the constituent elements of the church can and must be present within the house church. The recognition of this fact is the unique and revolutionary character of what is happening in Halton today. For most of the other similar developments (including the famous Methodist "class meetings") have until now not so radically attempted to show forth all the constituent elements of the church as was the case in the early church and as it is being attempted now in Halton.

Before exploring how the different constituent elements of the church can be shown forth in the house church, it is important to define more clearly what we mean by the term "house."

The "House" Today

The New Testament term for "house" (*oikos*) designates first of all a place, the place where people live and work. The house church therefore is where people actually live and work.

It is important to note that already in the New Testament the meaning of the term *oikos* is not restricted to the house as a building. Very often it rather means house in a social context. *Oikos* then becomes almost synonymous with "family," "tribe, " or the concrete social environment of a person. This broader sense of the term must be kept in mind when we say that in early Christian times the church lived and spread "by houses."

But where is the *oikos* of modern man? It is no longer necessarily and exclusively the "home" of his postal address. For most men and women in industrialized societies the "house" of residence and the "house" of work have fallen apart. Family ties have been loosened. The rapid social change and the growing mobility which characterize modern society foster the disintegration of the old fabric of group life and constantly create new patterns of living, new "houses." The church does not a priori know where the *oikos*, the concrete social context of modern man, is. Therefore, the church has first to discover that *oikos* without any preconceived ideas about the value of different social structures. And just as Christ came to man where he actually lived and worked, so the church has to go to modern man in the concrete context of his *oikos*.

Because of the very differentiated and mobile structure of modern society there is not just one, but many types of "houses": it might be the street in a new housing area or the factory in a disintegrating rural area. And many persons will have more than just one main *oikos*.

The church's task is to build up house churches in these different "houses" and the modern parish or local congregation should be the organic union of such house churches. This, however, is almost impossible for the parishes and congregations as they are now, because usually their area is identical with an administrative unit which formerly may have been a real unit of social life, but which today cuts right across the many and manifold "houses." Such sociologically outdated parishes and congregations can no longer integrate the different house churches. Therefore, some house churches tend to become para-parochial Christian communities and sects, cutting themselves off from the larger community life of the church universal, while the old parishes and congregations are constantly being deprived of their best members. The restoration of the cellular structure of the church, through building up house churches, therefore necessitates structural changes in the traditional parish and congregation system of the church.

II. The Constituent Elements

If the house church is church in the full sense of this word, the constituent elements for the house church are the same as for the church in general. There is no universally agreed list of constituent elements of the church, but the four elements mentioned in Acts 2:42—fellowship, apostolic teaching, prayer, and the breaking of the bread—would certainly constitute the bulk of such a list. How are these four elements shown forth in the house church?

Fellowship

No church without fellowship. The very first task of the church universal and the local church is to live out this life of community. But there was seldom a time when this fellowship of the Holy Spirit, this common life in the body of Christ was of such a crucial importance as today. According to E. W. Southcott, "Maritain has said that every age has its relative pattern of holiness and the relative pattern of holiness for today is community. The church is the community."[4]

But the sad truth is that the general breakdown of community and communication which characterizes our time has also deeply affected the life of the church. Only in the Pentecostal and other more or less sectarian movements, this new third major type and branch of Christendom, has the Christian community fully adapted itself to the extreme mobility of modern society. Community with mutual sharing is provided and therefore the proclamation of these movements—even if it is a distorted one—has the necessary "sounding board" which makes these movements grow so astonishingly both inwardly and outwardly.

In fact, it is mainly in small groups and in the realm where people live and work together—thus in and through the *oikos*—that the church as a whole and the individual Christian grow. In studying the New Testament passages about "growth in Christ," one will soon discover that none of them speaks about growth in isolation. No man is "in Christ" by himself, but always together with others. For growing into Christ means growing into the body of Christ. In discovering the primary significance of group dynamics for the growth of personality the modern group psychology has only rediscovered what Christians could have learned long ago from the Bible: we can become ourselves (i.e., real human beings, children of God) only through the other—alone I am not myself. It is in the other person and through my relation with him that I grow. The early Christian gatherings therefore did not consist of a star-preacher speaking to a church public listening in a huge hall; Christians came together to devote themselves "to the apostles' teaching and fellowship, to the breaking of the bread and the prayers" (Acts 2:42). In such gatherings which for the most part took place

---

4. Southcott, *Parish*, 17.

"in homes," everybody could participate, "each one has a hymn, a lesson, a revelation, a tongue, or an interpretation" (1 Cor 14:26).

All those who have participated in meetings in house churches and similar living Christian community-groups testify that this fellowship with its possibility for mutual sharing is the greatest contribution made by the house church to the building up of Christ's church on earth. No fellowship without discipline. In the same chapter where Paul describes the fellowship meeting of the Christians, he adds that "all things should be done decently and in order" (1 Cor 14:40). That is only the outward discipline. Yet living Christian community-groups need still another discipline which orders the life of the group members individually and the life of the group as a whole. Some groups have been led to a rather strict personal commitment, while others were led by the same Spirit to abstain, for the time being, from any explicit commitment and rule of life. But all the groups discover the need for some kind of "ordered life" and stress the importance of the promises and commitments made at baptism and reaffirmed at confirmation.

A Fellowship of Learning

In order to grow in Christ, Christians have not only to devote themselves to fellowship but also "to the apostles' teaching." But it was a great error of the Western world and of the churches in the West to separate too much the (Christian) education from the living (Christian) fellowship. One has to live among illiterates where there are not yet any schools in order to understand fully that the best "school" is the natural life-and-work community.

And a comprehensive Christian education can best be given in a small group and preferably right within the natural life-and-work community, thus in the house church.

Here lies the great importance of Bible study and all other study work done in the house churches. Here at the frontier situation, meeting in the dispersion, the members of the church learn together to become adult Christians: they are learning to see the great facts of redemptive history, revealed in the Bible, in the context of daily life and work and the needs of the society in which they are living. Here they are learning to lead by leading, they are learning to pray by praying together. In short, the house church is the way in which the people of God learn to be the church in the world.

A Fellowship of Prayer

The house church is a means to exercise the common priesthood of all believers. And one vital element in this common priesthood is prayer. Many of the different Christian cell movements actually began as prayer groups.

In Halton the house churches developed out of the prayers offered for each of the ninety-nine streets of the parish for more than ten years. But now this prayer is not always done in the church building. When the congregation meets by the dozen in dispersion in different homes and different parts of the parish the prayer for the streets is continued in a more concrete and direct way; streets become families and families become persons.

When a person is ill, the church of his street will not only pray for him (and return thanks if he has recovered), but the church will visit him in order to pray with him. The minister and the people of God in his street will bring him communion and join together in the laying on of hands. Through this healing ministry many a home with a sick or crippled person has become itself a power center of the fellowship of prayer and healing.

Prayer and healing: these two things belong together. It is astonishing to see how in most of the house church and Christian cell developments, sooner or later the question of the healing ministry of the church is raised.

> We need bands of people who are prepared to meet in the church building or in homes to pray for those who are sick. . . . We need, above all, to help patients' relations and friends see their vocation as healers, to see their vocation to surround the sick-bed with faith and prayer and not with hopeless or stoical sorrow . . . [for] the church is a healing fellowship.[5]

A Eucharistic Fellowship

The very heart of the Christian community is the holy communion. Wherever we meet this community, be it in a church building, a prisoners' camp, or an ordinary home, we can and should find also the celebration of holy communion. It is the firm belief of most Christian churches that at every communion service, at whatever level, the whole church is celebrating: there seems to be no valid theological reason against the celebration of holy communion by a small number of Christians (through an ordained and authorized minister or priest) at any time and place.

5. Southcott, *Parish*, 122.

In Halton the home-celebration of holy communion has become the key to the whole development of house churches. "There is nowhere that our Lord incarnate would go that our Lord in the holy communion wouldn't go. So, let us take the Eucharist back into life, let us build up the church in the house."[6] During the week regular home-celebrations are held in the homes of the confirmed members of the congregation. Each celebration includes a short sermon, which links these home worship services with the worship service of the whole congregation on Sunday morning, because on Thursday, Friday, and Saturday the congregation meeting in the dispersion looks forward in the sermon to next Sunday's collect, epistle, and Gospel respectively, and on Monday, Tuesday, and Wednesday it looks back in the same way. Besides these regular home-celebrations there are special celebrations in the homes of those whose child has been baptized; in the homes of the sick; in the homes of the candidates for confirmation; in the homes of the nonconfirmed in order to help them see something of the meaning of communion, even though they cannot receive the sacrament; in the homes of those who are going to be married or who have just been married. And E. W. Southcott even says that "the long-term policy is that all baptized people should have a communion service at their burial." "It is as the congregation becomes aware of itself as a eucharistic fellowship that communion will be seen as the 'done thing' . . . at all the great events of life; . . . it will be seen as the way to keep the Sabbath holy, and to keep the whole of life holy, to put God in the center of life, and in the center of the world."[7]

III. Let the Church Be the Church

This was the slogan at the beginning of the modern ecumenical movement. Since then the ecumenical movement has indeed more than once become a means whereby the Holy Spirit has helped the church to be more truly God's church on earth. The mission, unity, and renewal of the church (and their interrelatedness) are becoming more and more the focal points of the ecumenical discussion. Has the house church any relevance to these matters? To what extent is it a way to express and foster the mission, unity, and renewal of the church?

---

6. Southcott, *Parish*, 59.
7. Southcott, *Parish*, 123, 124.

The Mission of the Church

The house church is definitely not just another evangelistic weapon, a technique for getting at those who could not be reached otherwise. T. Ralph Morton is right in fighting against the conception of the house church as merely "the next step" after visitation evangelism and evangelistic mass meetings. He writes: "The house church represents a first step in finding a new direction for the life of the church. The danger is that we welcome it as a next step on quite a different journey and dismiss it because it is so slow."[8]

The house church is in fact a way of building up a missionary church, a spontaneously evangelistic community. Mission becomes here not so much a separate, specially organized activity, but a spontaneous *rayonnement*.

The fellowship of the house church which does not exist in a Christian ghetto but in the midst of the different "houses" of modern society becomes in itself the greatest missionary factor. For—to put it in the terms of Prof. H. Kraemer—there can be no "communication-of" without "communication-between."[9] We cannot preach the gospel to outsiders. Christ himself did not preach from the outside. First, he became man, and was with us in the world. When the church meets in the dispersion, especially when it meets in the homes of "outsiders" (as it happens in the "extensive house church meetings" in Halton), there is a chance that Christians may come in contact with such outsiders, listen to their real questions and problems, and through this listening ministry create a common world, a "communication-between" which will open the way to "communication-of" the Good News.

The fellowship of prayer will soon become a fellowship of service. Where house churches or other living Christian community groups have developed, the church's *diakonia* has been remarkably renewed. Loving service becomes the concern of the whole congregation. The church meeting in small groups in the dispersion knows the needs of every street, it knows the way to help, and it is there to help. Everybody who has studied the history of missions knows that such spontaneous, loving service is another great missionary factor. The fellowship of learning will be "ready always to give an answer to every man that asketh . . . a reason" concerning the hope that is in them (1 Pet 3:15). As soon as the church really appears as living Christian community groups within the natural groups of society and as a fellowship of serving action, the astonished "outsiders" will begin to ask

---

8. Morton, "House Church," 5.
9. Quoted in Weber, "Church in the House," *Laity*, 48.

questions. And now the Christian fellowship becomes quite spontaneously a witnessing fellowship; this fellowship is not "illiterate" with regard to the Biblical message! Within the context of the living Christian fellowship and service the spoken word has its necessary "sounding board." It is spoken "with authority." It becomes a real witness, instead of degenerating into a shallow declamation, giving perhaps right answers to questions which are no longer asked or at least no longer addressed to the church.

The eucharistic fellowship is constantly reminded, in the celebration of holy communion, that there can be no false separation between the sacred and the secular, because our Lord takes our ordinary daily food and drink as a means whereby he continues to recreate, redeem, and renew. And the breaking of bread reminds us that Christ's sacrifice is for the world. When the holy communion is celebrated within the real "houses" of society, the terms "secular" and "world" are no longer pallid, abstract terms, but quite concrete realities. Here the eucharistic fellowship has to become a missionary fellowship.

During the first Christian centuries the church lived not only "by houses" but it spread "by houses." We are told that a certain person was baptized "with her household," "with all his family" (Acts 16:15, 33; 1 Cor 1:16). Recent developments in mission and younger church areas—especially the group movements in India and elsewhere—have shown us that we must recover this group approach and free our traditional mission work from Western individualism. The same plea is made also by those who stand on the evangelistic frontier of industrial society in the West. The "house church" is an answer to this plea.

The Unity of the Church

It is a great gift of God when many members of the pilgrim people of God are allowed to meet one another from many traditions, countries, tongues, and races—as happens in the big ecumenical gatherings—or from nearly all the cities and villages in one country—as happens at the German "*Kirchentag*." It is a great gift, that God has set apart a day (and here we might add now: a church building!), so that the Christians in one place may come together for the Sunday worship service, for the parish meeting and the parish meal (the Biblical *agape*). But these occasions are the exception, for, during this time between Christ's ascension and return, the people of God live mainly in the diaspora. This fact has not been sufficiently considered in the ecumenical discussions on church unity. In this time of the Christian diaspora the unity of the church has mainly to be shown forth in the life of the people of God in the dispersion.

It is in the different "houses" of society—be it a street, a factory, or any other concrete life-and-work community—that Christians have to recognize one another. Here they have to be a fellowship, although a "fellowship of the dispersed," as Melanchthon said. "See how they love one another": this was one of the testimonies pagans gave to Christians during the first centuries. E. W. Southcott tells us how the house celebrations have helped to restore such a fellowship: "The force of the invitation to confession often comes home more seriously round a kitchen table than in the bigger parish communion congregation. Neighbors who have fallen out and who have come quite comfortably to the church building, have seen that they cannot attend a house-celebration in their neighborhood without first healing the break."[10]

This questioning leads the "fellowship of the dispersed" to become a fellowship of learning. For, in meeting Christians from other churches and traditions, one soon discovers that one's own church lacks wholeness. We begin therefore to learn from one another and to share together the fragments of truth each of us has received both individually and through his church. In Halton there are now regular interdenominational house-meetings, where Christians from different denominations continue to learn from one another.

These interdenominational home meetings were an outcome of the "Week of Prayer for Christian Unity." The fellowship of prayer would soon be hypocritical if, in praying for one another and with one another, there were no readiness and deep desire to learn from one another, to endeavor to give united witness and service and to grow together, in the place where the dispersed people of God live and work. It is in this setting of daily life and work, in the different "houses" of society, that the eucharistic fellowship experiences most intimately its unity (when sitting as a small group round a family table for the holy communion) and its disunity (when the celebration of the holy communion becomes impossible in an interdenominational home-meeting). In fact, it is at the "house" level that "the challenge of disunity comes with fresh force. Where most of the superficial differences disappear and men of the same household still find themselves divided, the

---

10. Quoted in Weber, "Church in the House," *Laity*, 50.

'why' and the 'how long' press with more insistent reality."[11] It might therefore well be that the house church will be the point where the Lord will give his church the precious gift of visible unity.

The Renewal of the Church

When, at Evanston, the churches which had covenanted in the World Council of Churches dedicated themselves to God anew, praying "that He may enable us to grow together," they knew that this search for visible unity means to be changed and renewed "through crucifixion and resurrection." Similarly, when studying their mission and recognizing that this mission can only be accomplished by an "evangelizing church," they saw that the very first step in accomplishing this mission is the "renewal of the inner life of the church." No advance in the mission of the church and no visible unity of the church without a continuing renewal of the church!

The renewing power is the power of the Holy Spirit. This power is not given to isolated individuals, but to persons who, at baptism, are incorporated into "the fellowship of the Holy Spirit." The dynamics of the Holy Spirit are therefore intimately linked both with the renewal of the church and with the living Christian community groups. For this reason, there is a deep inner relationship between church-renewal and living Christian community groups: Church renewal happens not first of all in and through individual Christians nor in and through larger units of the church, but mainly in and through small cells of the church.

IV. The Whole People of God

It is no secret that most churches suffer from the evil of clericalism. However, the remedy for this illness is not the anti-clericalism which characterizes so many lay movements, but the recovery of the whole people of God, the *laos*, which comprises both the laity with their ministry in the world and the office-bearers with their specific ministries. All those who have participated in the life and work of house churches testify that the house church has led them to exactly this recovery of the whole people of God, where the layman becomes a real layman and the pastor a real pastor. "In the house church we have discovered the meaning of worship and mission

---

11. Robinson, "House Church," 304.

with fresh reality and relevance, and in it we are discovering the need for a new kind of layman and a new kind of ordinand."[12]

Learning to Be the Church in the World

The task of Christians is not to do something for the church but to be the church. Most Christians think they know how to be the church on Sunday morning when the people of God are assembled on church premises. But most Christians are at a complete loss when it comes to being the church on weekdays when the people of God are dispersed in the world. The house church is an answer to this frustration, because here the actual life of the church members becomes the content of the church's life. T. Ralph Morton observes rightly that

> at present for most members of the church there is a clear division between the things the church deals with and the ordinary concerns of its members. There are certain things you talk about in church buildings or are talked to about. There are the things you talk about on the church steps or in the passages. And they are not the same. When the church meets in the house the division breaks down. The house church cannot escape dealing with the ordinary concerns and anxieties of men and women. . . . It is here that the real obedience of men in their daily lives will be worked out, very slowly.[13]

Sharing Christ's Priestly Ministry

One of the theoretically most cherished and practically most disregarded heritages of the Reformation is the Biblical doctrine of the universal priesthood of the people of God. The house church is a way to practice this universal priesthood. Laity and office-bearers join together in visiting the sick, the elderly people and the lonely, in the whole teaching task of the church as well as in the healing ministry in the widest sense of this term, becoming thereby a redeeming community within their particular "house."

In this exercise of the common priesthood the office-bearers have the task of preparing the different house churches for their priestly task in their "house," guiding and sustaining them in the fulfillment of their reconciling ministry.

---

12. Quoted in Weber, "Church in the House," *Laity*, 53.
13. Morton, "House Church," 5.

Sharing Christ's Prophetic Ministry

Many sermons and most of the declarations and statements of synods and world councils—intended to be a prophetic voice, bringing man under the judgment of God and proclaiming the good news to him—are hopelessly dull. They do not touch the heart because they are general messages to the church in general, or general answers to general challenges.

Many exceptions could of course be quoted. But the fact remains that actual people (to whom a concrete prophetic message can be given) and concrete challenges (which can be met by a concrete prophetic answer) are mainly encountered on the "house-level." Therefore the church can fulfill the major part of its prophetic ministry only through house churches: here the laity (members of the people of God, who spend most of their waking hours in a "worldly" occupation and who are therefore "specialists in worldly affairs" in the church) and the *"verbi divini* ministry" (this title for those who have been set apart and trained academically to become theologians means literally "the servants of the Word of God") are searching together for the timely prophetic word (or silence!) and the right prophetic action and attitude in the concrete setting of the "house."

In this exercise of the prophetic ministry the office-bearers have mainly the task of becoming theological partners and theological teachers within the people of God. A theologically sound statement or action is of course not yet a prophetic action; theologians need the "specialists in worldly affairs" and both need first of all the power of the Holy Spirit in order to become prophetic. But on the other hand, the whole people of God, and especially lay people who are engaged in the world, need theology in order not to be "tossed to and fro and carried about with every wind of doctrine, by the cunning of men, by their craftiness in deceitful wiles" (Eph 4:14). They must learn to discern, judge, and decide theologically, i.e., to see and handle the small and large problems of their daily and professional life in the light of God's design and his plan of salvation. Through the service of the theologians among the office-bearers, many laymen and laywomen have to become "lay theologians" in their house-communities.

Sharing Christ's Lordship over the World

Christ's lordship over the different "houses" of society becomes effective through the obedience of the members of the people of God living in these "houses."

We have already seen that it is mainly in the living Christian community-group meeting in the frontier situation where the real obedience of men in their daily professional and social life is slowly being worked out. There the church learns to become the church which functions as salt and as light.

It is quite obvious that those members of the people of God who spend most of their waking hours in a "worldly" environment and occupation, i.e., the laity, have the main responsibility in this sharing of Christ's lordship over the world. The special task of the office-bearers is to hold constantly before the whole people of God the claims of God, his great redeeming acts which evoke our response of obedience in faith.

The Perfecting of the Saints

Christ "gave some to be apostles and some prophets and some evangelists and some pastors and teachers, for the perfecting of the saints unto the work of ministering" (Eph 4:11).

This is "the new kind of layman and the new kind of ordinand" who is being rediscovered in the house church. The laymen and laywomen are called to be saints: to live a holy life in the midst of the world (herewith making "whole," i.e., "healing" the broken relationships in their particular "house"), to go "the way of the Lord" in the midst of the labyrinth of modern society (herewith giving direction, purpose and hope to man in despair).

In order to build up and equip such "a royal priesthood, a holy nation, a people for God's own possession" (1 Pet 2), Christ gave his people "apostles," "prophets," "evangelists," "pastors," and "teachers." Theirs is this special function of building up, equipping, and perfecting the people of God. We have known this for a long time—in theory. The development of the house churches is a way to practice it.

4

The House Church in the New Testament[1]

Quintus Leatherman

It is quite clear from the New Testament record that early Christians worshiped in houses. Not only were prayer meetings held for special occasions, but from the very beginning we find "the breaking of bread from house to house" (Acts 2:46). Here we have a constituent element of a church in effect—"the breaking of bread." Here was a distinctively Christian worship, apart from the temple prayers, held in private houses because there was no other available place of meeting. "The earliest supper-celebrations took place in the course of the evening meal—expressing a symbolism that their meal was a continuation of their fellowship with Jesus. It was a meal in which they felt themselves closely united to Him."[2]

> The leadership of the "Apostles' teaching" was destined eventually to draw the church away from "the prayers" of temple and synagogue into a distinctive order of worship. The heart of that worship from the beginning lay in "the breaking of bread"; and the breaking of bread was the central and characteristic action of the "*Koinonia*" as the common life of the church.[3]

It is generally agreed by New Testament scholars that Acts 2:42–47 describes the constituent elements of early Christian worship. The translation of verse 42 is now generally accepted as rendered "in the teaching of the

---

1. Excerpt from a Seminar Term Paper on the House Church.
2. MacDonald, *Christian Worship*, 60.
3. Thornton, *Common Life*, 332.

Apostles and in the fellowship."[4] The *Koinonia* (fellowship) was something apart from the apostles. It is a participation in the Holy Spirit which all had together in common. It was not so much that the Holy Spirit was the subject who brought them together in fellowship but rather as the object in which they all shared. Teaching and instruction were important elements in the early Christian worship service.

Prayer was an important element in the worship of the primitive church. While in the initial period they also attended the "prayers" in the temple, they "continued" in their prayers in the homes. Probably the order of service was relatively free and spontaneous as is indicated in Paul's description of a worship service in 1 Cor 14:26.

New Testament evidence is abundantly clear that houses were used as centers of Christian worship. In Jerusalem, the house of Mary continued to be used as such after Pentecost. As the number of believers increased, more houses were used as centers of worship. The suggestion is clear in Acts 12:17, that when Peter returned from prison to the house of Mary that James and the brethren were already gathered in another center of worship. The church in the house of Priscilla and Aquila are twice mentioned in the letters of Paul (1 Cor 16:19; Rom 16:5). Rom 16 mentions Christians by groups with an indication that each group had its own meeting place ("And the brethren who are with them . . . and all the saints who are with them"—vv. 14 and 15). Paul addresses Philemon and the "church in your house" (Phlm v. 2) and Nymphas and the "church in her house" in Col 4:15. Furthermore there were many households (*oikos* or *oikia*) which became the nuclei of early churches, e.g., the households of the Philippian jailer and of Cornelius the centurion. The household or family of Stephanas in Corinth were the first converts in Achaia and apparently devoted themselves to the "service of the saints" (1 Cor 16:15). The Greek word *oikos* meaning house is also used in a figurative sense to indicate a household or family in the case of Cornelius and the Philippian jailer. Again, we have this same word used figuratively in referring to a body of Christians or the church in Heb 3:6—"We are his house," and in 1 Pet 4:17—"The household of God." In 1 Tim 3:15 the identification is complete—"the household of God, which is the church of the living God."

It is also a historical fact generally accepted that formal places of worship, churches or temples, were not erected until late in the third century. There are various literary references to the existence of homes for worship

---

4. Hopwood, *Religious Experience*, 222.

and teaching during the second and third centuries. In the Clementine Recognitions reference is made to the generosity of Theophilus of Antioch, "who with all eagerness . . . consecrated the great palace of his house under the name of the church."[5] A large number of Protestant scholars share the traditional Roman Catholic view that the Church of St. Clement in Rome stands on the remains of a house which was the first-century house of Clement of Rome. It is no doubt true that the early Christians found the house the means of having a distinctively Christian worship and fellowship from the very first days of the Apostolic age while they continued connections with the temple and synagogues in order to win their fellow Jews to an acceptance of Jesus as their Messiah. These relations were severed after the persecution of Stephen (Acts 8:1). Persecution by Jewish leaders and later persecutions by the Roman emperors made the household the natural locus for the meetings of fellowship and worship among the believers. As Filson states: "It was the hospitality of these homes which made possible the Christian worship, common meals and the courage-sustaining fellowship of the group. The Christian movement really rooted in these homes."[6]

The significant part played by house churches and households in the early church is revealed in the great attention given to family life in the letters of Paul and in the General Epistles. "Paul, speaking pointedly to the husbands, wives, fathers, children, masters, and slaves concerning their duties, realized that the Christian tree would be known by its fruits in home life and particularly in the life of the home which housed the church. A pertinent question would naturally arise. Would not the ministry of the church to the home be more effective through the medium of the house church?"[7]

In summarizing the significance of the early house churches, Filson states:

> It thus appears that the house church was a vital factor in the church's development during the first century and even in later generations. It provided the setting in which the primitive Christians achieved mental separation from Judaism before the actual break occurred. It gave added importance to the effort to Christianize family relationships. It explains in part the proneness of the Apostolic Church to divide. It helps us to gain a true understanding of the influential place of families of means in what has

---

5. Filson, "Significance," 107.
6. Filson, "Significance," 109.
7. Filson, "Significance," 110.

sometimes been regarded as a church of the dispossessed. It points us to the situation in which were developed leaders to succeed apostolic workers. Obviously, the apostolic church can never be properly understood without constantly bearing in mind the contribution of the house churches."[8]

---

8. Filson, "Significance," 112.

5

Can the Adult Sunday School Class Be the "House" Within Which the True Church Is Experienced?

Paul M. Miller

The Search for Renewal Today and for "the Church within the Church"

The revival of interest in the early Christian "church which is in thy house" is only one aspect of a larger search. The search for renewal of vital life within the primary, face-to-face groups of the local church is one of the most promising in-breakings of the kingdom of God in our time. Many Christians see it as the "cloud the size of a man's hand" upon the horizon. Monographs upon the essential nature of the church increase in quantity and quality. The raw individualism of both Neo-orthodoxy and Fundamentalism have failed to discern the church as Christ's body, within which the believer is covenanted, not only to Christ in a vertical relationship, but also horizontally to his brother within the covenanted community. There is a search for an "incarnational theology," a love-community which will function together as Christ's body upon earth now, and whose total life together demonstrates and gives meaning to Bible words like grace, forgiveness, redemption, and faith.

The search for renewal and for the covenanted group who will pilgrimage together under the cross is further prodded by the obvious fact that the modern church is so pathetically irrelevant to the day-by-day problems of the common lives of its members. Christians look to the state for creative leadership in grappling with ethical issues. They lean upon secular insurance agencies rather than upon brotherly mutual aid to help them in times of trouble, and to secular therapists rather than the brother-to-brother priesthood of believers to help them with emotional problems requiring confession, insight, and a deeper faith.

The dream of a "fair millennial morrow" or "the Christian century" to be launched by a social gospel, Christianizing the great social institutions of society, has been given a rude awakening and disillusionment. It has become painfully obvious that neither individuals nor institutions can be redeemed and transformed by any diffused glow of religiosity. Too often Christianity is finally equated with middle-class respectability and one's own pet panacea for political reform.

Secular researchers rise up on all sides to stab the slumbering conscience of the church awake. They are discovering that modern man needs most desperately just those things which the church would be supremely fitted to supply, if she would have the courage and the humility to really be the church. Sociologists point out that, when vital group life fades out in a local community, then moral standards deteriorate. When a community deteriorates into a "dust heap of unrelated individuals," something tragic happens to the individual person. Anthropologists point out that man becomes bewildered and insecure when his supporting primary group relatedness decays. Group dynamics researchers amass evidence which shows that real creative change within personality occurs through responsible sharing in group decision. Psychologists of personality point out that man needs to live within a covenant of love, that he needs a sense of core worth, that he needs self-transcendence and a way to take upon himself his own finitude and face death in faith, that he needs total acceptance, that he needs a therapy group where he is loved as he is with non-judgmental love and thus is free from his defensiveness and free to mature. He needs to feel that he can begin to communicate about the deep, unutterable concerns of his existence with other persons, and he needs a sense of vocation which comes as a call from destiny.

The church is uneasily aware that, if she would recapture the total sharing and obedience of the little group which gathered around the feet of Jesus, if she would deliberately seek to have members become members one of another at a deep level, and if she would ask members to bring their total existence and resources under the service of God's kingdom—then the church could meet the basic needs of man, could again carry the real meaning of history within her bosom, and could again cause the world to cry in astonishment, "Behold how they love one another."

The Deeper Meaning of "the Church Which Is in Thy House"

Some searchers are suggesting that, if the gathering of believers were again transferred to the homes of members, some of the intimacy of the primitive apostolic church might be recaptured. It is hoped that there, amid the scenes of common daily concerns, Christian faith might again seem more relevant to daily living.

However, the modern tiny bungalow does not lend itself very well to the need for Sunday school rooms, if graded study is to be provided for all members of the families that gather. The deeper problem is whether the modern one-family bungalow is or can be anything near the oriental household within which early Christianity spread and worshiped. The house then was a large cluster of rooms, with an entire clan, consisting of many uncles and cousins, with a central court large enough for the entire clan to assemble. The modern bungalow is not usually next door to the parents and cousins. The house then was often the center of common economic activity. It was the factory where men went to their jobs. The modern "priests in industry" movement are urging that man's real *oikos* or "house" is actually in his factory where the real center of gravity of his life is. The household in oriental life was also a cell of mutual aid and burden bearing. The modern bungalow knows little of communal sharing beyond its own immediate family. When the church spread "in thy house" within oriental culture it meant that it emerged where man's total existence was lived. Christ asserted his claim right where economic, social, and personal issues converged. The church needs again to plant the church at the center, the converging focus of man's total existence, but it is a serious question whether this is accomplished by the simple device of starting house churches. The Christian home may well continue to strive to give to its children their first experience of "church, " where all of life is brought under Christ's lordship, but the modern home cannot fully and finally be the Christian church.

What Is Required for Any Group to Consider Itself the Church?

Is the mere proximity of two or three Christians sufficient to assume that the church has "happened"? If a small group gathers for study and confession and search together for God's highest, can they say that they are the church? Those who believe in sacramental grace believe that partaking of the sacraments creates the church. Luther added that sharing in preaching and sacraments causes a group to become the church. The non-liturgical Christians are not very clear as to when a group dare conceive of themselves as being the church. Is every activist group the church who gather to report on their individual accomplishments in passing out tracts or Bibles, serving for relief, or saving souls? Is a group necessarily the church because they band together as a team to hold tent meetings and engage in other forms of evangelism?

There are certain things which the church is, in her essential nature, as she is being created by God's Spirit. Only when a group expresses the essence of the nature of the church, can that group consider herself the "church within the church." Groups which do not attempt to express together all phases of this essential nature should not think that the church has happened in its full reality, just because they are near one another.

When God's Spirit creates the church, he creates a believers' group, sharing the same vows of faith, response, and commitment to Christ. Unless a group consciously shares the same vows of personal discipleship to Christ, are they the church?

The church is further the *ekklesia*, the binding-and-loosing meeting of heaven's citizens. Conscious of their citizenship in heaven, they meet in a citizens' meeting to bind upon earth those things already bound in heaven. This responsibility to practice mutual discipline and brotherly rebuke, even to excommunication if necessary, flows from the essential nature of the church, and no group unwilling to bind themselves to practice obedience to Christ as individuals and as a group should think of themselves as fully the church.

The church is further the household or family of God. Here a *koinonia*, a closeness and concern, exists as Christians realize that they are God's family and children. They are members one of another in ties and kinship which transcend earthly ties of relationship. A deep sense of mutual obligation must exist and needs to come to expression in mutual aid and burden-bearing. It is questionable whether a group of Christians unwilling to become members one of another until "when one member suffers all suffer," should claim to really be the church. The group needs to feel that God's Spirit who is creating the body of Christ and family of God will give the charismatic gifts needed to enable the group to function as Christ's body. Individual gifts will be heightened, and abilities enriched by God's Spirit so that members of the group who are covenanted to one another can adequately serve and meet the needs of one another. There is a very real question whether the church has really "happened" until the group has begun sacrificial mutual aid. If this is relegated to government welfare and secular insurance companies by the modern Protestant church, she has sacrificed a vital part of her very essence and existence.

The church, as God creates her, is the salt and light to sub-Christian society. She needs to get on a lampstand and shed the light of God's truth upon the darkness of social issues. She needs to permeate society as salt and prevent decay by her very presence and prophetic witness. Until a group has taken up its task as the conscience of society, is it fully the church?

Finally, the church is the people of the living God, responding to his covenant of grace to them by adoring worship. A group needs to actually be the "community of memory and hope," refreshing by sermon and symbol God's redeeming and revealing deeds and words in the past. In group worship the people assembled before Jehovah offer the fruit of their lips giving praise, as a sacrifice acceptable, they present their bodies a living sacrifice to God as a part of every worship encounter. They gather for group worship and dialogue with God, expecting God to reveal his person and will through the testimony of the brother in whom he dwells, through Scripture and sermon, and through nonverbal symbols such as communion.

In view of the above statements as to the essential nature of the church, it follows that every group of Christians which happens to be together for search or fellowship should not claim to be the church, unless the group is really expressing the essential life of the church as she calls men to belief in Christ, engages in mutual discipline to safeguard obedience to Christ and separation from the world, practices mutual aid, speaks prophetically in God's name to the sins of sub-Christian society, and engages in corporate worship. If a small group within the church does fulfill these requirements so that it can consider itself the "church within the church," it should not depreciate the place of the great congregation or of the entire church of the Lamb.

Can Adult Sunday School Classes Become "the House" in Which the Reality of the Church Emerges?

The adult classes of our Sunday school already have some of the essentials for the small face-to-face group which can become "the church within the church." The groups are small enough so that each can share and feel his responsibility and allow the charismatic gift God's Spirit has given to him to be released in service to the group.

Because the Sunday school class is primarily a community of search for God's will while gathered around his opened word, the group can be saved from the doctrinal subjectivism which has plagued Moral Rearmament and other renewal groups. The Sunday school class is closely tied to the Bible; it is not merely relying upon numinous truth or subjective feelings.

If the adult Sunday school class could be made up of parents who live as neighbors in one part of the parish, then the class could have as one of their chief reasons for existence the evangelism of lost persons in their neighborhood. In laying a loving strategy to make the warmth of Christ's love as felt in their fellowship to flow around their unsaved neighbors, the class could be expressing again the essential nature of the church.

If the adult Sunday school class is made up of parents from a given area of the parish, the group could also recapture the sense of community responsibility so sadly fading in our society. They could then relate their study of God's word to the need for justice and righteous living in their neighborhood. They could engage in mutual admonishing and rebuke as they attempt to bind and loose and practice disciplined holy living. They could seek to actually be the salt and light to their community. If our adult Christians do not now feel a sense of responsibility to be the salt in their community, they must be led to do so.

Then, too, if the adult Sunday school class of parents from a given neighborhood wish to further be and express the essential nature of the church, they can engage in mutual aid and burden-bearing as an ongoing class "project." Since they already are neighbors, they can know one another's needs and thus bring their total existence and shared, common concerns under the attention and ministry of the group. The group can become the real bearer of pastoral care to members, rather than expecting a solitary pastor to deal with everyone in a professionalized, one-to-one relationship.

By having husbands and wives from a given neighborhood thus sharing in study, mutual rebuke and discipline, mutual aid, evangelism, and prophetic witness, the church can make her life vitally relevant to the home life, the community problems, and the daily lives of members. By engaging in all these activities together, the adult Sunday school class can recapture responsible membership and the involvement of Christians in the lives of one another. The Sunday school class can then be the "house" of shared existence in which the church is experienced.

There are still other advantages in seeking to have the adult Sunday school class become the cell of the church's homogeneous life. Because it is an existing face-to-face group it can offer continuity with the historic church. It will be better able to avoid exclusiveness than is likely if the cell of renewal is formed around common-interest or hobby lines. It can more easily avoid a "holier than thou" attitude if it is an ongoing unit of the existing church, rather than a self-conscious group of persons who seek out their own type and regard themselves as the real leaven of the kingdom. If it is tied to the sobering task of evangelizing their part of the parish it can avoid the comfortable retreat to some mountaintop to build there three tabernacles. It can more easily avoid the pitfall of becoming a mere self-improvement society which is intent upon saving its own life and so loses it. If it has old and young parents from one area in a class together, it can more truly be a cross-section of the church which is made up of old and young and needs both. If a Sunday school class really tries to meet the needs of all the diverse type of families in a given part of the parish, the group will be driven to explore the breath of the gospel's appeal and relevance. It is not so likely to become a clique of elite intellectuals who converse in terms common people cannot understand.

Conclusion

The church must be planted in man's "house," his *oikos*, at the place where his life concerns converge. If there is now no such converging point in man's life, then the church should help provide one and insist that the church assert Christ's claims for total loyalty there at the center of man's existence.

The church must express her essence in the interaction of small, face-to-face groups, where all can become totally involved and committed to one another and together to Christ . Every lasting surge of renewal during the history of the church was carried forward in small class meetings or other primary groups and it must be so now. No amount of hearty backslapping or experiences in the mass meeting can be substituted for this.

To really be the church, a group must experience and express obedience to Christ, which separates the group to a disciplined, separated life; evangelism which is harnessed to an actual soul-saving task close at hand; mutual aid in which all suffer when one member does so; group worship experiences, and a serious attempt to become salt and light to the community.

If a burning desire to experience the full reality of Christ's living church can be instilled and inspired in professing Christians, until they are willing to pay the price in study, prayer, and obedience—then the adult Sunday school class of parents from a given community has every possibility of becoming the "church within the church." It is better situated to avoid the pitfalls which beset the "cell" movement than many other new groupings which might be formed. If the earnest desire and obedient search are lacking, no new grouping will succeed either.

It is better to begin where the church actually is in any search for renewal than to insist upon bypassing the already existing face-to-face groups in the local church and encouraging other groups to form in search of renewal. Christians will find themselves distracted and their home life further weakened, if they attempt to be loyal to the existing calendar of essential church activities, and then in addition set up another series of gatherings of cell, prayer, or search-for-renewal groups. The average congregation is not so dead or corrupt that it is time for awakened souls or souls seeking God's highest to withdraw their most vital interest and support from the existing prayer meetings and Sunday school classes. The average pastor is not so closed to God's renewing work in the church that he needs to be left high and dry with the deadwood of the membership and the calendar of activities while those who desire God's highest set up other activities as rivals for the faithful worker's time.

Finally, the Spirit of God must be sovereign. He must be allowed to blow where he wishes, and the church must ever remain sensitive and obedient to his desire to break through in new forms. If the existing forms will not contain a mighty new ferment of the Spirit's working, then it is time to get new wineskins. But before anyone concludes that the adult Sunday school class cannot become the face-to-face group within which a new and mighty ferment can yet work, he owes it to himself and the church to give it a thorough and fair trial.

These suggestions are offered as a contribution to the ongoing conversation and search for renewal within the church and are not to be regarded as an attack upon any existing "cell" movement. It is readily admitted that merely reshuffling the adult Sunday school classes so as to have husbands and wives from a given area of the parish meeting together, will not automatically give to them the passion to evangelize their mutual neighbors, to bear one another's burdens in mutual aid, to be the conscience of their neighborhood by "salty" living and prophetic witness, or to share their total existence and common lives as a community of spiritual gifts. It is only asserted that these challenges to really be the church must be held before all Christians constantly and that the adult Sunday school class members who wished to commit their lives to a search for obedience and spiritual renewal would find their Sunday school class situation ready and waiting as a nearly ideal channel to express their obedience to Christ.

6

Group Dynamics in Evangelism (by Paul M. Miller)

A Review Article

ALBERT STEINER

Miller, Paul M. *Group Dynamics in Evangelism*. Scottdale: Herald, 1958.

In the book *Group Dynamics in Evangelism*, Paul Miller gives an inspirational and challenging recast of much of the recent study in the field of group dynamics. This new field (the combination of psychology, sociology, and psychotherapy) studies the unique and therapeutic values of small groups. It reports that small groups may actually be more effective in some areas than any single expert working with the individual.

The writer has applied the findings of group dynamics in areas of therapy, group decision-making, and leadership in the evangelistic work of the church. He shows from the findings that the group by its multiple, yet individualized, influence can be more effective than the single leader or the crowd in confronting life's problems and inadequate personal attitudes. There is a deeper contact between real personalities in the small face-to-face group than in the crowd that may temporarily have its attention focused by a leader or an issue.

The book is organized mainly around the functioning of small informal discussion groups; it studies why groups disrupt, how leadership is acquired and exercised, and what are the functions of the other roles within the group.

The writer has rendered a real service by gathering material from various sources that are not usually available, presenting it in summary fashion, and interspersing it with applications to the work of evangelism.

In addition to the general applications throughout the book, there are two chapters on the uniqueness of Christian interaction. First, drawing from his own and others' experience, Miller discusses the plus element of communication possible between "transparently honest" Christians because these people can approach each other in the Spirit of Christ with great depth and penetration. The last chapter undertakes the difficult task of making a few of the applications of this knowledge to the congregational life of the church.

The core of this book calls attention to the resources which dedicated groups within the church can and should contribute to the evangelistic life of the congregation. He shows a unique place for the function of these groups—enveloping nonmembers with concern and love within the context of their interaction so that they can be drawn into Christ.

As is natural, the book raises new questions for the church to answer. The writer, of course, could not cover everything. He leaves unanswered the problem of the formation of these groups—where they can come from—what activity or issue can become their formation center. Within the book, the assumption seems to be that already functioning groups can be used, and he suggests a progress record to evaluate the evangelistic effectiveness of these groups. In his article in *Concern* No. 5, Miller has also suggested geographic Sunday-school classes as a place of focusing evangelistic responsibility.[1]

But the awkward question still remains: Where or how do we find, nurture, or perhaps create the type of group that can in a self-giving way help the non-Christian to meet the living Christ and find an effective life in Christ? Most groups do not measure up to the high standard of selflessness which is outlined for the evangelistic group interested solely in others. We know our selfishness and the times we have revolted against God. How can members who basically want to be less self-centered and bound by their own needs, prejudices, and irritations, develop or be developed into the transparently honest, hopeful, and loving people who can accept others in the state they are and yet call them beyond this into new life?

What then can a searching group of Christians do, either as they continue in a group to which they already belong or in a new one? To meet

---

1. Miller, "Can the Adult Sunday School," essay in this volume.

solely as an evangelistic body often becomes either a farce or an impossibility. Since seekers are often frightened by a group which is "out to get them," the evangelistic group would tend to play-act at some other activity. But in the process, they would become hypocritical. The example is given of the birthday party in which the Spirit did work as a group of Christians had fun together but also shared their experiences in Christ.[2] Perhaps part of the answer is to be found in the normal sharing, giving, and receiving of admonition and participation in the life in Christ, in the life of the obedient church. Perhaps the contagious joy of growing and living is the most effective call to new birth in Christ. This would mean an honest facing and resolution of the dividing disagreements that continually arise in any group seeking to have all its members exercise their Spirit-given gifts.

The book shows that the implications and challenges of small informal discussion groups are a valuable resource that the church must use. The challenge is now to discover and encourage the unique activity of these groups within the already functioning structure of the church.

2. Miller, *Group Dynamics*, 177.

7

Evangelism Through the Dynamics of a Christian Group

GERALD C. STUDER

In preparing this topic, I have struggled long and hard with the problem of bringing order and presentableness out of the opinions and convictions that were storming my mind and heart. On the one hand, I have read and studied within the context of ten years in a rural pastorate. On the other, I have constantly come across ideas that thoroughly intrigued me, but which must now be presented without having given them much of a trial, if any.

Let me begin by making an attempt at describing what seems to me to be a fairly typical Mennonite congregational program. This program operates in a context which can perhaps be best described as ambiguous. If ambiguous does not describe the situation, it at least describes our fogginess in understanding it. This congregation has 180 members and many small children. Half or less of this congregation's wage-earners are farmers. The other half are anything from businessmen or factory workers to schoolteachers and office workers. I believe that in the best sense of the word, this congregation is an average congregation. There is to be found in it the same range of consecration and problems that any pastor of a medium-sized congregation falls heir to. There is the same type of program that many other Mennonite congregations have. There is the weekly Sunday school, morning worship, and a Sunday evening Young People's Bible Meeting followed by a preaching service. There are midweek prayer and Bible study services for adults, children, and young people. These midweek services are attended by an average of from one sixth to one fourth of the membership. Beside these, there are class meetings, boys' and girls' clubs, chorus practices, Mennonite Youth Fellowship activities, summer Bible school, two series of evangelistic or Bible conference meetings a year, weekend conferences, and the like.

In checking the membership book of that congregation for parents who are now active in the congregation, I learned that forty-three of their children are either lost to Christ and the church entirely or else hold a nominal membership in some denomination other than our own. In reviewing the annual pastor's reports for the past number of years I discovered that they had barely broken even in gains and losses. Almost all gains were from within the brotherhood. A few persons had come their way seeking a church home but have either gone on again because the congregation was unable to absorb them (due to a divorce problem, for example) or else they were finally dissatisfied with what they found. An attempt was made to win the lost of the community through a two-by-two evangelistic visitation program. This resulted in about six pairs of members responding to the challenge presented by the pastor. The effort produced one convert among the elderly people of the community.

I tell this story of a congregation because of what I am about to say. I am convinced that, even though this picture is as common as I am led to believe it is, and as dark, Dwight E. Stevenson is realistic and constructive when he says:

> We have to start where we are with what we have. This means that the polarities and tensions of the existing churches must be endured if we are going to penetrate the shell of institutionalism and of human self-righteousness and get at the kernel of community. This does not call for dreaming dreams and seeing visions as much as it calls for Christian realism. The kernel of Christian community is always present in the existing churches. All we have to do is recognize it and nurture it.... Where, then, is the Christian community in a local church? It is there within the existing institution, among the people who are actually present, waiting to be recognized and released to do its work. It does not wait for some other building, or for a new form of organization, or for a change in membership. It is not a utopian community. It is a real community of real people in a real situation—and this means in an imperfect situation, for people are human.[1]

---

1. Stephenson, "Only Christ," 11.

I believe we are all agreed that the way to get to where we want to be and ought to be is to start from where we are. The status quo might be ever so cleverly, and even accurately, described as "the mess we'ez in" but it remains nevertheless that it is not hopeless if God is in it. Space does not permit an analysis of the church and a description of the reasons why the congregational programs so familiar to us all are missing their mark today. I trust that we are open to the possibility that we do not merely need to improve and increase our evangelistic efforts but that we may also need to consider seriously the need for renewal in our congregations. I trust too that we need not enter into the debate as to whether a congregation of 180 members can be a church. We need not deny the word church to a larger congregation in order to enlarge the word church to include the two or three who gather in Christ's name. It is this latter aspect of our church life that we have lost, and it is this aspect that I want to discuss.

A discussion of the dynamics of a group for evangelism does not require a rejection of other means of evangelism, such as mass evangelism, radio evangelism, literature evangelism, and others. I am inclined to believe, however, that the small-group method comes nearer to being the best evangelistic method than does any other now in common use among us. The distribution or proclamation of the gospel to the masses may produce the "nibbles" necessary in our fishing for men but the evangelistic task is not done until we have "landed" the Lord's catch. Even the landing of the Lord's catch does not fulfill our evangelistic obligation, for we are to teach them "all things whatsoever I have commanded you." This is a lifetime job.

It is quite obvious that group life was one of the distinguishing marks of Christianity in the apostolic age. One can scarcely imagine a bridge club or a sportsmen's club eliciting the comment from the casual bystander, "Behold, how they love one another!" This was an exclamation of amazement at the presence of something new in human relationships. It was noticed because these believers were interacting in a way that was heretofore unheard of in so secular and sophisticated a society as that of the Roman Empire in the time of our Lord, and after. The lives of church people still elicit comments from non-Christians, but it is regrettably seldom that it is this kind of a comment!

To be impressed with the potentialities of a group for evangelism, we need only recall that the church began in a group of twelve called by their Master "to be with him, and to be sent out" (Mark 3:14). We further remember that when Jesus wanted to spread his name and gospel abroad, he sent out first the twelve and then the seventy in groups two by two. The whole founding and spread of the Christian church is to be largely described, if not explained, in what Hans-Ruedi Weber has called "the rhythm of retreat and re-engagement." This rhythm recognized by our Lord and used with such ultimate effectiveness in the accomplishment of his own purposes suggests at once what the two major purposes of the church are to be, namely, spiritual growth through group fellowship and the spreading of the gospel. I am so convinced that these two aspects of the Christian life comprise the lowest common denominators of spiritual life, the without-which-there-is-nothing, that I am about prepared to assert that any group or institution that operates without both of these is not a church.

André de Robert has written that "there is much hidden significance" in the fact that Jesus sent forth his disciples two by two. This significance is more and more believed to lie in the direction of the basic meaning of the church. Dean Henry Alford considers the verse in Matt 18 which says, "Where two or three are gathered together in my name, there am I in the midst of them," a generalization of the term church and the powers conferred upon it. Many of us have thought this verse meant "two or three are enough. You don't need twenty or thirty," but it would seem rather to mean "One is not enough."

However, the specific mention of "two or three," while it is not accidental, is not the heart of the matter either. While a revival of interest in small groups is in itself a symptom of and a solution for the impersonal, mass character of our society, yet even firsthand human association does not necessarily exhaust the meaning of this verse. Indeed, it may sidetrack us from the real point entirely. The uniqueness and the importance of this verse is not simply to encourage the more intimate association of people, but its purpose is to bring people together in such a way, and in order, that Christ may be in their midst. Is it too much to suggest that Christ is in the midst when two or three have gathered in his name because it is his church that has met, and the body is not complete without his personal presence and headship? This is precisely what E. H. Plumptre seems to believe about this verse, for he says: "The true meaning of the words is well embodied in the well-known patristic axiom, *Ubi tres, ibi Ecclesia* (where three are, there is a church). The strength of the Christian society was not to be measured by a numerical standard, but by its fulfillment of the conditions of its life. The presence of Christ was as true and mighty, his communion with his church as real, when his followers were but as a remnant, as when they were gathered in the great congregation"[2]

It may be suggested that this verse had particular relevance to a time and place in which Christianity was illegal but that today the "great congregation" is God's will. I do not believe it is a matter of one or the other, but it does seem that today's church would point us back once again to the realization that the church is somehow more vitally realized in the intimacy of a small group than it can ever hope to be realized in a "great congregation. " A. B. Bruce comments on this verse also and says that the number two is "not the measure of Christ's expectation of agreement among his disciples, but of the moral power that lies in the sincere consent of even two minds. It outweighs the nominal agreement of thousands who have no bond of union."[3]

This leads us to our next step: that not only is the church most genuinely present in the small group, but it is in such a group that Christ is best able to call the lost unto himself. We believe that "the church is not only the fellowship of the redeemed, it is the redeeming fellowship." That is to say, evangelism is to be the fruit of Christian fellowship, both horizontally and vertically. Just as there is no evangelism that does not begin with a disciple's commitment to the Lord, so there is no evangelism that can ultimately involve only this vertical relationship. Jesus Christ has ordained that his gospel should be spread abroad by the church, the two or three together, going forth and proclaiming his name.

This is not to overlook the fact that Christ has and does honor the attempt of a lonely witness with evangelistic success but it is to give due recognition to the fact that Christ always sent his disciples out two by two and that even after he had ascended into heaven, his first great act on behalf of the evangelization of the world was the calling and consecrating of two of his disciples, Paul and Barnabas. Perhaps Halford E. Luccock's conclusion is worth our careful consideration when he said that "all great movements in Christianity have been based on the training of small groups."[4] The occasion of the sending of these two missionaries seems to have been the meeting together for prayer and worship of some half-dozen early church members. John L. Casteel has reminded us that "the genius of the Methodist movement

---

2. Plumptre, "Gospel," 113.

3. Bruce, "TO KATA MATΘAION," 240. It should be noted that this original article title misspells the name of Matthew's Gospel; it should be MAΘΘAION.

4. Luccock, "Gospel," 7:686.

which enabled it to conquer the raw lives of workingmen in industrial England, and the raw lives of men and women on the American frontier, was the 'class meeting'—ten members and their leader, meeting regularly for mutual encouragement, rebuke, nurture, and prayer."[5]

Did not our own beloved Mennonite Church spread by houses? And was it not so because it had recovered once again a basic New Testament principle of evangelism? Few things are clearer than that the reason for the reported daily growth of the early church and for its "having favor with all the people" was due to the fact that the believers continued daily with one accord "from house to house" breaking bread and eating their meat with gladness and singleness of heart. Paul speaks again and again of house churches and it is not at all clear that the fact can be lightly passed by as though it were only an accident. Develop technologically as we will, we may be quite certain that the most fundamental needs of human nature are not to be altered. There is a vacuum in the hearts of men that is in the shape of God and that vacuum will not be filled until that person finds reconciliation with God and that fellowship with other Christians that invariably flows from such a divine encounter. No individualism, or fragmentation of men into compartments of secular and spiritual, will long be able to even pretend to fill that spiritual vacuum. God has made us to share with him, and with others in him, all that we have and are. This need can be concretely worked out only in the intimate fellowship of a small group. It may find substantial satisfaction in the family, but it is doubtful that it will find full satisfaction there.[6] It is strange indeed that we Mennonites have so lost or are so late in rediscovering this whole concept of both the church and evangelism. It would seem to be obvious that a concept of a believers' church would have utilized largely the type of intimate spiritual fellowship which only adults can enjoy. Would not the recovery of the small worshiping, evangelizing group go far in helping us recover the concept of a committed band of disciples? Can you imagine ten- or twelve-year-olds being attracted to this type of church the way they are to a church which operates so largely on mass appeal and "staged" services? It would seem that the splitting of the present institutional church into atoms or cells of spiritual life and evangelistic outreach would nevertheless

---

5. Casteel, "Introduction," 20.

6. Note the further testimonies to the need for the rediscovery of fellowship in "The House Church: Something New?" section of Weber's "The Church in the House," essay in this volume.

still need to retain its mass meetings for the purposes of larger group worship, teaching, preaching, and the business and administrative affairs of the congregation and denomination.

> Where but in a group can we become aware of our responsibility for each other, and of the prodigal journeys that we rush off on from time to time? Unlike the thieves in the ancient story, in a group we cannot go off and leave our wounded man half dead—we have to keep meeting him time and time again in most intimate quarters. Nor does the man stay wounded along the road, awaiting our beneficence. No, he is not lying on a hospital bed needing the gracious chaplain, nor is he a person in deep trouble turning to the trusted counselor. He is often a cantankerous adult whom we deeply resent; and he comes, not to seek help, but to stab us in public. In such situations is the battle for one's very soul fought when we risk membership in a group.[7]

These are the words of Ross Snyder who does not write as though he were anyone to dream up new theories or techniques of evangelism. He writes as one who knows from personal experience how we need to be saved from many things long after we have accepted Christ as our Savior and Lord. He knows that one of our most needy fields for evangelism and personal encounter with Jesus Christ is to be found right among the members of our churches. But more than this, he is equally aware of the appeal that such a group would have to the "outsider." He further writes:

> We can participate in another's life or in a joint life with him, only upon his invitation. We cannot force our way in; the hand that opens the door to the depths of another person will always be on the inside of the door. But we can reveal our nature so that he will come to want to open the door, so that transactions may take place. People sense and respond to the spirit revealed in John Woolman's resolve: "a concern arose to spend some time with the Indians, that I might feel and understand their life, and the spirit they live in; if happily I might receive some instruction from them, or they be in any degree helped forward by my following the leadings of truth among them."[8]

In all our mass evangelistic meetings, it is taken for granted that any seeker will not finally and fully be helped until he has been taken into the

---

7. Snyder, "Members One of Another," 9.
8. Snyder, "Members One of Another," 8.

confidence of a personal worker and/or the evangelist. We simply know that people do not really remove their masks and face others and themselves in honesty before God and their fellow men without the grace and spiritual strength that only God gives. We further know that it is only in such a condition that a person can find that blessed release from sin and the joy of the Holy Ghost. And so it is that while the Holy Spirit may convict people of their sin and need of a Savior in mass meetings, he succeeds in bringing them to Christ in the small groups of an adjoining room. The church of the Saviour in Washington, DC, believes so strongly in the necessity of a small group for the leading of the Spirit that they assert dogmatically that "no man can be a Christian by himself" and arrange their life together as a congregation, whose active spiritual life is lived in a dozen or more small groups of six to ten persons each. This brings us back to the place where we began, namely, how to relate all this to the practical life of our rural or urban congregations.

I am fully aware of the fact that I have only opened the subject, and that in a rather rambling and certainly incomplete manner. Perhaps you have noticed some statements which you believe lack evidence in their defense or are only partially true. I would like now in closing to tie the loose ends together by recommending that we give serious consideration and prayer to the potentialities for evangelism and personal growth that is to be found in the small group meeting in Jesus's name.

8

Small Congregations

Virgil Vogt

Small congregations need to be established within our large congregations in order that the work of the church may be carried on most effectively.

Four articles in *Concern* No. 5, including this one, are united around a common theme: the house church. I believe it is the conviction of all the writers that we must rediscover in our own time the way in which the church can live and work "in thine house."

The term "house church" is derived from a New Testament phrase in which the term "church" is used to describe a gathering of believers which met in a particular home.[1] However, the term "house church" does not mean much to the average American and often is completely misunderstood.

Perhaps, therefore, our thesis could better be stated thus: that the establishment of a number of small congregations to function within the large congregation offers significant opportunity for church renewal and a growing participation in the world mission of the church. Almost without exception, this proposal seems to provide a practical and constructive way for the local congregation, as it now exists, to come to grips with the critical issues which have such a devastating effect on the vitality of its life at present.

The phrase, "small congregations to function within the large congregation," has the distinct advantage of showing: (a) that the small group is exactly identical in nature and essential character with the large group, and

---

1. Rom 16:5; 1 Cor 16:19; Col 4:5; Phlm 2.

(b) that the small group and the large group can and must exist in functional unity with each other, and not independently.

The Grounds for This Proposal

In addition to the New Testament passages which mention "the church in thine house," we also find the term "church" used to describe a Christian congregation encompassing an entire city, thus: "the church which is at Corinth." In the New Testament the concept of church was equally applicable to the small house-congregation or to the large city-wide congregation. Not only did the believers share in the life of their own "house church" but they also shared in the life of the church throughout the city (Acts 20:17).

The New Testament church gives us a picture of small and large congregations existing simultaneously in the same place and with the same members. The closest parallel in our own time is the simultaneous existence of the local congregations and the district conference, each complementing and helping the other to carry out the work of the church.

However, the impetus for "small congregations to function within the large congregation" does not come primarily from the pattern of church life which can be observed in the quotations cited above, although these are important. But in a much more profound sense the impetus derives from what the New Testament says the church is. The very nature of the church and the essential character of its existence are more involved in this suggestion than a particular form of church order which we see reflected at certain points. While the latter is important, the former is more important.

And besides all this, the impetus is derived from our own experience as churches today. It is not simply that we think the Bible says this is the way the church should live (important as this may be) but in addition, we have discovered for ourselves that the church really loses its vitality if it seeks to live in any other way.

This is a large affirmation. How can it be supported? How does this proposal for "a number of small congregations to function within the large congregation," really grow out of the essential nature of the church?

In a general way, I think one can fairly say that this proposal sustains positive relations to every aspect of the life and work of the church. Some of the other papers in this series have tried to show this.

But above and beyond what has been said, it seems to me that this proposal sustains an especially significant connection to that aspect of

Christian experience which has commonly been referred to as "discipleship." The small congregation has the potential for being especially creative in restoring the relevance of faith to life and making grace operative in the everyday crisis of our existence.

The Congregation in Its Hearing and Doing

The significance of this point can perhaps be most easily understood if we use the twofold division of Christian experience which is often employed in the New Testament, that of "hearing" and "doing" (Matt 7:24; Jas 1:23). In modern theological lingo it would be revelation and response.

"Hearing" refers especially to that aspect of Christian experience by which we become aware of God's action, his self-revelation to man. We become aware of what God has done in other times and in other places. We listen to a proclamation of the righteousness of God which has been revealed in Christ. We study the Bible to see and understand God's redemptive work. We seek to discover how God has reconciled the world to himself, and how he plans to sum up all things in Christ. In all of this we are observers and listeners—it is the process of "hearing" God's word to man.

The necessary counterpart of "hearing" is "doing." The revelation of God has no meaning for us until matched by our own response. "Doing" refers not to God's action in other times and in other places but to God's action here and now, in our own particular circumstances and with our cooperation. "Doing" is that process by which God's redemptive work becomes contemporary. What was potentially accomplished at Golgotha finds genuine expression in our own time and circumstances. As by faith we take our stand in the stream of God's redemptive history, all that has become known to us in the process of "hearing" now becomes a part of our own experience through "doing." We are identified with it by our response.

The entire life and work of the church can be understood in terms of this twofold cycle. First there is revelation in which the church comprehends God's redemptive history. Then there is response, as the church turns to its own immediate situation and makes certain decisions and acts which are consistent with redemptive history and which grow out of the church's unique place in this unfolding drama.

Doing as a Task of the Church

What we have sometimes overlooked, however, is that both "hearing" and "doing" are church tasks. These are matters which need to be worked out by the whole congregation, as Christ exercises his lordship through the functioning of various gifts. Members of the body of Christ are dependent upon the Head and upon one another, for a proper fulfillment of either the "hearing" or the "doing" of God's word.

The general tendency has been to neglect "doing" and give the bulk of our attention to "hearing" God's word. We have built-in provisions for teaching and the proclamation of the word. The whole church works together to make sure there is a "hearing" of the word.

No matter how poor the congregation, if you go there on Sunday morning there will usually be a sermon. No matter how impoverished the spiritual life of the congregation they usually work together for a "hearing" of the Word through the Sunday school instruction.

But in contrast to this, we have made little regular provision for the congregation to work together with equal diligence to affect a contemporary response which is worthy, consistent, and in rapport with redemptive history. The congregation provides many practical activities, to be sure. These are usually optional. And at no point is the entire response of the individual seen and evaluated in its wholeness. While "hearing" is understood as the task of the whole church, what should happen in respect to "doing" is left almost entirely up to the individual. There is no built-in arrangement for combining the contributions of all the members for this task of "doing" God's word so that the experience of each member is seen in its totality and in its relation to the whole.

In preaching and teaching the individual discovers what it meant to be a Christian in the first century. The instruction may even become more practical by the use of modern illustrations to show what it has meant for other Christians in our own day. Very rarely, however, does the congregation seek a united definition of what it means for us to be Christians.

To work out the meaning of faith in our own particular circumstances is a task left for the individual. Some guiding principles are set out, to be sure, and the individual also has the counsel of his friends, be they Christian or non-Christian. But the church as a congregation usually does not function in this phase of the twofold cycle of "hearing" and "doing."

We readily recognize how weak and impoverished the life of the church would be if each individual were left to seek out his own private interpretation of the Scriptures. If there is to be a true "hearing" of God's word, then the congregation must take responsibility for it. The responsibility of the individual is not thereby done away with, rather it is strengthened and complemented by the work of the entire congregation.

The church takes corporate responsibility to make sure we understand the circumstances of redemptive history, past and future. Is it not equally important that the church take corporate responsibility for understanding the circumstances of redemptive history in its present dimension—our own lives in the light of God's word?

Indeed, it is often easier to reach agreement and understanding about what it meant to be a Christian in the first century than to agree and understand what it means for us to be Christians in the twentieth century. The questions of discipleship may be even more difficult than the questions of hermeneutics.

Thus, it seems to me, the task of the Christian church remains unfinished until she has turned from a proclamation of the eternal gospel of redemption, to address herself, as a church, to the specific details of her own contemporary situation—till she spells out the meaning of faith in terms of her own membership in all their complex relationships, in terms of their time, their money, and their personal resources. If Christianity is to have any meaning for us, then it must make a difference in all of these practical concerns. And it is the task of the church to help us discover what that difference is.

But when we come to deal with the contemporary situation, we must deal with particular people whose names we know, with specific problems and real situations. We must move from general principles and the realm of theory to specific cases and the realm of action.

In discipleship we must come to grips with the particular situations that confront us and deal with them in the light of the Christian faith. So in view of our foregoing discussion, the church which is really faithful to her whole task, including both "hearing" and "doing," is the church which not only proclaims God's acts, past and future, but also provides a time and place for the congregation to consider particular cases in which the meaning of Christian discipleship in our own time is not clear. The congregation needs to work together to help each member reach Christian decisions in some of the many knotty practical concerns of our time. The church must not only speak about Biblical characters and what it meant for them to be Christian, but it must also speak to its own membership and about what it means for us to be Christian. And this speaking to its own membership needs to go beyond vague generalities to concrete situations. Anything less than this is not enough.

Now, it is just at this point that "a number of small congregations to function within the large congregation," might be taken up in the experience of renewal. By re-ordering the life of the congregation so that individuals become functioning members of both small and large congregations at the same time, the church once more has at least the opportunity to deal creatively with the practical issues of discipleship. The small congregation is small enough (ten to thirty members perhaps) so that individual cases and problems can be taken up by the congregation, while, on the other hand, it is still sufficiently large to offer the kind of objective judgment which the individual often lacks in appraising his own situation without any brotherly counsel.

Having the small congregation will not ensure that these questions of discipleship will be dealt with in a creative Christian manner, but it at least makes it much easier for this kind of question to be handled if the membership is so inclined.

The task of the church is to allow Christ to bring it together as a functioning body, with Christ himself as the Head and with each of the members exercising their own unique gifts for the upbuilding of the total church.

It is through the exercise of spiritual gifts that the church is built up and strengthened in love. Yet, to recognize and make way for the practical contributions of each member requires time spent in discussing and planning these matters.

One way for this to become possible is through the re-ordering of congregational life to include within the large congregation a number of smaller congregations.

The Nature of These Groups

In trying to distinguish what is being discussed here from the general trend toward small groups, and to define it positively, I would like to refer again to the phrase, "a number of small congregations to function within the large congregation." This gives us a twofold distinction, on which I will comment further.

The Nature and Essential Character of the Small Group Is Exactly Identical to That of the Large Group; Both are Congregations of the Christian Church

It is on this point, more than any other, that we need to take issue with the prevailing interest in small groups. Even where these groups are operating within existent churches, the small groups seldom exist as "church" in the full sense. Often when the term "house church" is used, the emphasis is more on "house" than on "church."

Canon Roger Lloyd, for example, in describing an English movement called the Servants of Christ Our King, specifically says they are not a church.[2] The same position is taken, either explicitly or implicitly, by the vast majority of those who have written in this field.

In the light of this prevailing tendency, it is of utmost importance that the small groups we are talking about here be understood as churches. And as such they must be distinguished from all the other small groups already existent within our congregations and elsewhere.

Any group which is not a church may be defined as a special interest group, for it lays hold of only one aspect of man's existence. It is only the church which lays hold of all aspects of man's existence.

We already have small groups within our congregations, which function in particular areas such as evangelism, prayer, fellowship, education, and service. The small congregation suggested here would have all these functions and more. The small congregation participates in the total work of the church—there is no question or problem outside its scope of interest and authority for action.

Some might ask, "Why is it so essential to insist that these small groups be churches rather than special interest groups?" The answer—to look for significant and continuing renewal through the work of a special interest group always represents a superficial analysis of the human situation. Only the church as the church is capable of undertaking such a great work as this.

The special interest group is formed to meet one particular need which may be especially pressing at the moment. If our witness has been weak, we set up an evangelism group, if our doctrine is weak, an educational group, and similarly other groups as needed for prayer, fellowship, or building.

While this procedure is useful and need not be set aside with the establishment of the small congregations, it has a fundamental limitation.

2. Lloyd, *An Adventure*.

This approach fails to recognize that while at the moment certain of our needs are more obvious than others, yet it is more correct to say that we have need in every aspect of our life under God. The forces of deterioration and breakdown are functioning in every aspect of the church's total existence, and there is only one group which is able to work on all the problem areas which need attention and to inaugurate and sustain genuine renewal, and this group is the church herself.

Special interest groups tend to overemphasize or under-emphasize their particular task, depending upon how faithful they are to the particular mandate upon which they are founded. The church, on the other hand, regardless of how small it is, stands for the whole cause of Christ—total work. If it is true to its own nature it will not emphasize one aspect as over against another, because all aspects belong to it and are an integral part of its life. The small congregation cannot set itself over against the large congregation, because even the large congregation is a part of its wholeness, and vice versa.

Another way in which this point becomes evident, is that special interest groups tend to lose their vitality when the particular problem which concerns them loses its urgency. Not so the church. For the church is the only institution in the world which is so constituted as to have relevance to every possible situation which may arise. It is a participant in the cosmic redemptive work of Christ, the Head, through whom all things in heaven and on earth are reconciled (Col 1). Thus, everything in heaven and on earth belongs to the work of the church, just as they belong to the work of Christ.

1. This means the small congregation should be active in witness and service among the unsaved and needy persons of the world. Any group which understands itself to be the church of Christ immediately takes upon itself the great task of world mission. Indeed, insofar as the group really comprehends what it means to be the church, they will see that they exist in the present time just for this purpose: to extend the redemptive call of God to all men.

    So every small congregation which is true to its essential nature will undertake this witness. It is integral to the life of the church and one of the questions which any congregation will need to face very early is this question of how each one of the members can become personally involved in the spread of the good news.

2. If the small group is a small congregation this means it should be active in strengthening and building up its own life of love. To do this involves teaching, proclamation, worship—"hearing" God's word. It also involves "doing"—mutual burden-bearing in spiritual and material concerns, brotherly admonition to recall those who are in danger of wandering from the truth, forgiveness for those who have erred but return in penitence. It involves the exercise of the gifts of the Spirit for the upbuilding of the whole church.

   If the small group is a small congregation, then the use of the Lord's supper, baptism, the recognition and commissioning of leadership—all these belong to the small congregation in exactly the same way as they belong to the large congregation.

   Obviously, however, where the large congregation and the small congregation live in very close proximity, a good practical way to take care of all these for both large and small groups will need to be worked out. In some cases, duplication will be necessary, in other cases not (this is dealt with again in a later section). But in either case we need to recognize that the small congregation has the same concern as the large congregation that each of these aspects of church life are utilized to fullest possible advantage within both the large and small congregations. Both the large group and the small group have the responsibility of taking action to achieve this purpose.

3. If the small group is a congregation, this means it should maintain a continuing conversation with the large congregation on significant issues and should always seek to maintain a unity in Christ. A few persons have expressed concern about the schismatic effect which small congregations might have within the large congregation. This, of course, is always a possibility, just as it is a possibility under our present system. But the point which is often overlooked is that maintaining unity with the church at large is an integral part of the total life of the small congregation. It is essential to its existence as a church. Just as the individual believer needs the church fellowship if he is to continue as a Christian, so the small congregation needs to cultivate and maintain a fellowship with the large congregation.

Many small groups and cells have had a schismatic effect in the church. In part this is due to a limited conception of their own role which allowed them to sever connections with the larger body without feeling any harmful effects to their own work. But the small congregation operates on the basic premise that its experience has relevance for the experience of other Christians, and the experiences of other Christians have relevance for it.

The small congregation which enters fully upon its own privileges and responsibilities will never accept two levels of Christian experience as a normal thing. Any significant differences which arise between the small congregation and the large congregation will need to be the subject of mutual inquiry before God.

Thus, the small congregation will share its own insights and concerns with the large congregation and the large congregation will share its insights and concerns with the small congregation.

This leads us to the second major point in our definition.

The Large and Small Congregations Can and Must Exist in Functional Unity with Each Other, and Not Independently

Several differing positions are brought under criticism with this statement.

On the one hand, there are some who contend that the small congregation and the large congregation are mutually exclusive possibilities. You cannot have both existing at the same place, at the same time, and with the same membership. This position, it seems to me, overlooks the witness of the New Testament, reflecting just this kind of situation, as well as the witness of our own experiences in congregations and district conferences.

On the other hand, there are some who would allow both small and large congregations to exist at the same time, but with no meaningful relations sustained between the two. Membership would be primarily in terms of one or the other. Membership in one group would have meaning, in the other it would be superficial. But this position overlooks the critical importance of unity within the Christian church.

Still others view the small congregation or "house church" as a temporary expedient which is to be employed until certain difficulties may be overcome and the life of the large congregation can be properly organized.

What I am suggesting here is that both small congregation and large congregation can exist together and function together. That wherever this situation develops it is important for both small and large congregations to include the other as an integral part of their own life and work. And finally, that this arrangement is not a temporary expedient, but an ongoing necessity of church life.

The large congregation needs the small congregation, as I have tried to show, because it is especially difficult for the large congregation to deal with the practical issues of Christian faith and life. Discipleship is apt to lose its meaning because the large congregation finds it impractical to discuss and resolve concrete contemporary problems.

The small congregation needs the large congregation to give its own work perspective, validity and support. Just as there are tasks which the large congregation cannot do as well as the small congregation, so there are other tasks which the small congregation cannot do as well as the large congregation. We need both.

The significance of the foregoing can perhaps be demonstrated best by seeing how this would influence the use of such important ordinances as the Lord's Supper, baptism, the recognition and commissioning of leadership.

As suggested earlier, there is no Biblical or theological reason why the small congregation should not exercise all of these within the circle of its own fellowship. However, significant practical difficulties may stand in the way.

Those who take the first position described above would say that these ordinances may be used in either the large congregation or the small congregation, but they cannot belong to both. Since they already belong to the large congregation, that leaves the small congregation empty-handed.

If those who take the second position are members of a small congregation, they would likely proceed to use the ordinances even though the large congregation stands in firm opposition to such an innovation. If they are members of the large congregation, they would likely tolerate the deviant action of the small congregation, even though flatly denying any validity for it.

For those in the third category, any use of the ordinances outside the regular program of the large congregation would be tolerated only as a temporary expedient.

The position advocated here is that the ordinances can be used by both small and large congregations if a functional unity exists between the two groups. Thus, when the one congregation uses the ordinances (or takes any action for that matter), this congregation is the agent of the other congregation and of the whole church. When one congregation acts, it acts on behalf of the other congregation and with its full authority. Thus, each congregation must recognize that action taken by the other has validity for it, and neither congregation is free, therefore, to use the ordinances in a way that undermines their effective use by the other.

When this inevitable interrelatedness is clearly seen, any action by one congregation to which the other congregation cannot subscribe will need to be taken up with utmost urgency, because the active congregation is, in fact, functioning as the agent of the other congregation.

The mutual relationship here is analogous to the relationship of husband and wife in their joint checking account. Unity of action is as much a concern here as when your wife is out writing checks for things which do not meet your approval. This position proceeds on the assumption that the small congregation belongs to the large congregation and the large to the small. There is a mutual interpenetration which makes it unthinkable for the two groups to take differing positions on such important concerns as these. Unity is imperative.

This means that members of the small congregation cannot begin to use the ordinances if the large congregation is opposed to this innovation. No innovations can be made unilaterally. There must be agreement on both sides. And where agreement is lacking, it must be cultivated.

Members of the small congregation are bound by decisions of the large congregation because they are also members of the large congregation. Members of the large congregation must recognize and respond to concerns of the small congregation because these people belong to its own membership. Christ is the Head of all.

So when churches function together, a plan of action can be set in motion only when it is mutually acceptable. To come to this unity may be a long and difficult task. To achieve unity may take much time, attention, and patience. But there is no other alternative. So long as the one who opposes us is recognized as a Christian brother we are bound, not only by our own convictions and insights, but by his as well. And it is in this light that one must work out a mutually satisfying plan for using the Lord's Supper, baptism, the recognition and commissioning of leadership.

Concluding Reflections

We began by suggesting that the establishment of a number of small congregations to function within the large congregation offers significant opportunity for church renewal and a growing participation in the world mission of the church. Then we tried to show why this might enable the church to be more creative in its present circumstances. It was also suggested that not just any small group but only the small congregation really has the potential for significant and sustained renewal.

In conclusion, we should note that strengthening and renewing the life of the church cannot be accomplished simply by using another practical gimmick or by making a few changes in our program. Unless the Holy Spirit moves us afresh then all else is empty form.

In many places today, I believe men are being moved by the Spirit. There is deep concern and a growing interest in the church in many quarters. A good number of these concerned persons, however, are overwhelmed by their situation. They know it's bad, they see its failures, they say something should be done. But they don't know where to begin.

The situation is often particularly difficult when the congregation involved has a large membership. "What can you do with a group like this?" they ask.

This entire proposal grows out of exactly that kind of situation. It offers a way to begin, even though the circumstances may seem difficult. If one is able to move ahead along these lines, then there emerges further opportunity to deal with other questions and problems of concern.

However, it should also be clear that this is not the only way to begin, nor is it necessarily the correct way in every case. If the pressing questions of faith and life can be dealt with within the existing congregational program, then let's begin there.

But whether here or there, let's begin!

9

Changing Forms of the Church and Her Witness

Leland Harder

One of the signs of the times in the continuing Christian movement in history is the current quest for new forms of the church and her witness. This quest is sufficiently evident and articulate to warrant analysis of its theological and sociological dimensions and to determine the character, consistency, and cogency of the solutions that are being offered to the problems of ecclesiastical function and order. This is the task to which the present essay is addressed.

It is somewhat misleading to speak of the quest for new forms, since the forms that are being sought or at least certain aspects of them are anything but new. Graydon McClellan hints at this embarrassment when he writes, "For years her prophets have beckoned, scolded, and cajoled, but the church has taken only timid and token steps to mount an effective city ministry; to integrate racially her membership and leadership; to enlist her congregations for aggressive mission: or to express the professed unity of the church in unified mission and ministry."[1] It is certainly worthwhile to ask whether and in what ways the forms which the church can take derive from the gospel itself, a question to which we shall return.[2] Nevertheless, both in Europe and in this continent, the "shape," the

---

1. McClellan, "Ministry," 123.

2. In this connection it is interesting to note that the Church of the Saviour in Washington, DC, which is certainly an excitingly new format for the urban church and her witness in our time, describes its *raison d'etre* in Christian primitivistic terms, as follows: "We are not called primarily to create new structures for the church in this age. . . . We

"form," the "pattern," the "structure" of the church has been the concern of a growing number of dissidents.

In some quarters the concern focuses on the "renewal" of the local congregation, that form of religious organization to which most Christians relate directly. This is typically a congregation located in proximity to the homes of the members, having an ordained minister, a churchly building, and a more-or-less self-enclosed program of worship, preaching, fellowship, and Christian education—much of which takes place on Sunday morning. This is a traditional form of church organization against which there is a widespread and growing reaction. The local congregation has earned this reaction, according to the editor of *Renewal* magazine, "by being a bore, by sanctimony and self-preening, by cliquishness, by dishonesty, by insipidity, by cleaving to the stereotype of the clergyman as a 'soft face over a hard collar,' by erecting monuments of stone in order to avoid encounter beyond the institutional fortress."[3] In other quarters, the concern focuses not on "renewal" but on "reformation," the assumption being that the existing structures of the local church cannot be renewed, but must be bypassed in favor of experimentation with new forms. We turn, then, to the examination of these inceptive movements of dissent within Protestantism, their indictments against the church, the options they present by way of remedy, their theological validity and maturity as judged from an Anabaptist point of view, and their implications for a vital evangelism and ministry for such a time as this.

The Indictments Against the Church

To say that there is a vocal and growing discontent with the established forms of the church in our day is to state a fact rather than to argue a thesis. The negative reactions to the church current in our time are coming at a point in American history when by all statistical indexes, the church is growing and booming. The disenchantment of youth in particular is not unrelated to this upsurge in church attendance and membership, for they with good reason ask whether mere attendance and membership in themselves are

---

are called first of all to belong to Jesus Christ as Saviour and Lord, and to keep our lives warmed at the hearth of His life. It is there the fire will be lit which will create new structures and programs of service that will draw others into the circle to dream dreams and have visions." See O'Connor, *Call to Commitment*, 94.

3. Rose, "Marks," 6.

criteria for the authenticity of the church. Unfortunately, some defenders of the established church look upon a question like this as a sign of rebellion and incipient apostasy.[4] They are beginning to launch a counterattack against the so-called "angry young men" who are leading this rebellion.

The identity of these "angry young men" deserves some comment, particularly with regard to their conceptual approaches. In all cases deserving of mention, they are men who are committed to the Gospel of Jesus Christ in its classical, historical meaning as the decisive Word of God to man in his wretchedness. The fact that some of them are professional sociologists is quite secondary as the source for their dissent. This comment is pertinent in light of a defensive counter-attack by Walter Wagoner, who observes that some of the most vocal among the rebels are sociologists. In a chapter entitled, "Sociological Thunder and Cultural Lightning," Wagoner writes as follows:

> One poll I should like to have taken in connection with this book would be "The ten writers who most influenced your seminary development." It is a sound bet that such a list would include at least two of the sociologists of religion: writers such as Herberg, Lenski, Winter, and Berger. By any intellectual litmus test, this school of writing has a powerful influence on most of contemporary seminarians. . . . A reading of contemporary sociology of religion, popular to the point of surfeit among trembling seminarians, is a maddening experience. Maddening in the same way that Freud is: too much truth for comfort and too much overstatement.[5]

After appraising not the sociological critiques themselves, but the formats of these critiques, Wagoner comes to the following defensive conclusion: "In reality, the body tone of American Protestantism is not so sluggish as to deserve the diagnosis being accorded it by the sociological Jeremiahs or by the seminarians."[6]

---

4. For example, Nels F. S. Ferre writes, "Nowadays it is fashionable to castigate the church. It is even considered proper for church leaders to cast religion out of the church. . . . Pumped full of prejudice against the actual church as to both its message and its life, this past summer I attended a variety of church services—small and large, in metropolis, city and village, and in several states—and each time I came away with a strong sense of the depth and reality of the worship and high quality of the message. It is time theological leaders appreciated and encouraged the good there is in the church. Scorn helps no one." "Theology," 1415.

5. Wagoner, *Bachelor of Divinity*, 18, 19.

6. Wagoner, *Bachelor of Divinity*, 23.

The proper assessment of this reference to "sociological Jeremiahs" requires at least the awareness that all four sociologists named by Wagoner have clearly differentiated between sociological and theological propositions. Their point of view would be approximately as follows. Sociologists, as sociologists, do not make judgments of value; they only make judgments of empirical fact. Moreover, even for the sociologist who is himself a committed Christian, sociological endeavor requires a willing suspension of belief, i.e., a willingness to admit for serious consideration the possibility that the truth of the matter is other than what we have been led to believe. This does not mean that values do not enter into the sociologist's choice of a problem to investigate, nor that the sociologist does not often make judgments of value which are informed by knowledge that has been gained by thinking scientifically: but when he does, he makes them by some other premise than that of sociology as a scientific enterprise.

The current quest for new forms of the church is a good example of how this works, for in their own nonscientific attitudes toward the church, sociologists may and often do take either a radical or conservative stance. As we proceed to discuss three forms which the current indictments against the church are taking, it will be noted that in the first case, a sociologist like Peter Berger takes a very radical stance: while in the second case, a sociologist like Frederick Shippey takes a conservative, institutionalized stance: and then again in the third case, a sociologist like Gibson Winter takes a radical stance. In the attempt to understand what the current quest for new forms of the church is all about, it is important to know whether the judgments which certain dissidents are making are essentially sociological or theological.

There are at least three major indictments which are being leveled at the church in the current literature on the shape of the church: and although these do not necessarily come from persons who share a common theological stance (as we shall see later), they may be thought of as three aspects of a common problem. One way of formulating the indictment is to say that the church has become an "establishment" or "institution" of the secular society. It took the courage of Franklin Littell and Peter Berger to speak of a religious establishment in America when the official dogma of our nation is that of thoroughgoing disestablishment and religious pluralism. "There are other ways in which churches can be 'established' besides the legal," writes Littell, "and when we set the present relation of American churches to our culture against the classical Free Church testimonies the painful question arises: To what degree are the American churches 'free,' and in what direction?"[7] Littell refers to the "Great Churches of America" series in *The Christian Century*, in which favorable publicity was given to "a mighty church" in Dallas, Texas, which took into membership eight to ten persons every Sunday, most of whom had never been seen or interviewed before.

> Whatever else we may say, these are the procedures and point of view of an established church. One is reminded of the protest of the Anabaptists against Hubmaier's practices at Nikolsburg (c. 1525), where fifty and sixty were taken in at a time without adequate preparation and without coming under the authority of the ban. The question arises whether, although legally "free," institutions with a promiscuous view of church membership are really Free Churches.[8]

Berger argues that, even in the legal sense, the church in America is an establishment. Not only is church affiliation a practical necessity for election to high office, not only does our military structure incorporate the church by commissioning and assigning chaplains to its regiments, not only are churches looked to by our government to assist by many ways in the enforcement of law, but the political establishment of religion means economic support as well. Berger suspects that the state-collected "church-taxes" that still support the church in some European countries amount to less in dollars and cents than the economic support which our own government gives to the churches through its tax-exemption laws. While official separation of church and state "implies the existence of a divorce" the actual situation "suggests a polygamous arrangement in which all wives share equally in the favors dispensed by the husband-state and in which there are careful rules to prevent any one wife from acquiring a position of special privilege."[9] As a result of this and many other accretions of the social establishment of the church in America which Berger analyzes, the church has rendered itself unable and unwilling to stand against the tides of conformity at innumerable points at which ethics for the Christian are at stake. Regardless of what we think of Berger's solutions to the problem, we have to acknowledge with admiration the way he makes Jesus Christ normative for ethics. He speaks forthrightly about "the decisive turning

---

7. Littell, *Free Church*, 68.
8. Littell, *Free Church*, 75.
9. Berger, *Noise*, 59.

point that occurs in a human life as a result of encountering the message of Jesus Christ."[10] He believes that the main problem of the church is "the effectiveness with which the religious establishment is designed to prevent the encounter with the Christian message."[11] Far from making Christ normative for ethics, the established church ratifies and sanctifies the middle-class values prevalent in the general community. This means that radical surgery is called for, and for those who take the Christian message seriously, it will mean a radical alienation not only in relation to the "OK world" but to its religious establishment as well.

A second indictment of the church in the literature to which we have referred is the success-orientation of the typical local congregation, which measures the degree of its effectiveness by statistical and financial indexes. When one reflects on the facts that one hundred million dollars are being spent monthly in this country on church construction and that the minimum with which a new congregation has to figure today in terms of a building campaign for a conventional church edifice is about $125,000, it is not difficult to predict what a budget geared to a building program means to a local congregation in which there is some concern for the quality as well as the quantity of membership. As soon as the "first unit" is constructed, there are the pressures of mortgage payments and maintenance expenses, to say nothing about the cost of supporting a paid ministry that is required by the membership of the typical congregation in order to have the kind of program that is wanted. The image of "success" that accompanies these conditions means an increasing membership, a rising budget, and an expanding program.

This image, moreover, predetermines the kind of church extension and missionary strategy that characterizes the majority of denominations in this country. Although "missions" is an item in the budget of most churches, it is assumed that a local congregation largely fulfills its missionary obligations by helping to support the ordained missionaries who are sent out by the denominational board and the denominational board in turn assumes that its missionary program will remain a matter of considerable subsidy for the years to come. This in no small part explains the scramble for "high potential" suburban sites for the starting of new churches which, by laws of ecclesiastical economics, will in five years be able to begin to share the burden of missions by proxy.

10. Berger, *Noise*, 114.
11. Berger, *Noise*, 115.

In this connection it has been illuminating to follow the debate on the criteria of the effective church carried on by the Department of the Urban Church of the National Council of Churches since 1955.[12] Aimed at discovering what is an "effective" church (the new synonym for "successful") these studies began with criteria gleaned from the urban church sociologists like Murray Lieffer and Frederick Shippey. In his book entitled *Church Work in the City*, Shippey put it on the line in ten points:

1. Reasonable membership size—at least five hundred active members in order to provide an adequate potential for a complete church life.

2. Proper Sunday-school enrollment size—at least matching active church membership; to produce and train sufficient Protestants for tomorrow's church.

3. Vital trends—growth of membership and Sunday school enrollment exceeding that for the population, percentagewise; to keep pace with the expanding city Protestant opportunity.

4. An adequate budget—at least a living salary for pastor and staff members plus a matching amount for benevolences; in order to procure a competent staff and to share in the work of Christianity around the world.

5. [Etc.][13]

David W. Barry, who is the executive director of the New York City Missionary Society, applied similar criteria to the task of the inner-city church: The task of the inner-city church is to be a successful church:

> I won't be evasive on definition of terms. I am talking about institutional success in terms of standards we all understand, and the criteria I would offer would be something like these: it ought to have somewhere around 350 to 700 members; in communities of newcomers, Negro or Puerto Rican communities or public housing project areas, the Sunday school ought to be the same size; the members should be contributing or raising something like $55 to $60 per member per year; it should have an active program at all age levels; it should have a full complement of volunteer Sunday school teachers and other leaders; and there should be some

---

12. See various issues of *The City Church* magazine from 1955, especially May–June.
13. Shippey, *Church Work*, 60–61.

evidence that it is deepening the spiritual life of those who participate, and making a difference in the community around it.[14]

As the debate on the effective or successful church developed, it was suggested with increasing urgency that any criterion of effectiveness implies a doctrine of the church. George E. Todd of the East Harlem Protestant Parish argued that if the church of today took the New Testament rather than modern American business as its model, it would be looked upon as a failure even as people looked upon Jesus as a failure. At this point the mediators began to speak of the debate as pitting a "theology of success" against a "theology of failure." George D. Younger, then minister of the Mariner's Temple Baptist Church in New York's lower East Side, reinterpreted the tension as being between "no theology" and a "part-theology."[15] All that Barry was giving in his essay was a sociologist's idea of a successful voluntary institution, which might—or might not—be describing a church of Jesus Christ, and in either case could not possibly provide the basis for a theology of the church. His criteria were no theology at all, even though they had a few theological overtones. Todd's theology of failure, on the other hand, expressed the incarnation and the crucifixion, but not the glad assurance of Christ's victory, both then and now, whenever Christians are gathered together in his name: thus, it was a part-theology.

The trend in the debate is a growing reaction to the use of the terms "success" and "failure" and an increasing stress upon the Christian mission as the standard by which the church should be measured. And by this standard the typical congregation of today is found wanting. As the editor of *Renewal* puts it, "There is little room in the churches for the person who feels that funds might be better channeled into active programs of service than into the construction of bigger and better church properties. . . . How many new churches decide *not* to build? . . . How many churches feel free to experiment, to follow the promptings of the Spirit, to try new ways of service, without sanction from their denomination?"[16]

The third way in which the indictment against the church is formulated in the current literature is its captivity to the sphere of residence and the insulation of the "residential church" from the expanding social settings in which the main drama of human interdependent existence is being enacted. The parish or "residential" church had some theological justification during

---

14. Barry, "Successful," 7.
15. Younger, "'Success' and 'Failure,'" 154.
16. Berger, "Whence the Rugged," 9.

the long centuries when the vast majority of the world's population lived in small rural folk societies, at the center of which might be the Christian church. Even the late Harold S. Bender in his address to the Conference on Mennonite Community Life could speak of the church and the Mennonite community as identical, protesting against "the dangerously unscriptural and un-Mennonite duality by which we so often draw a line between sacred and secular, between church and community."[17] The problem today, however, is that we no longer live in the relatively self-contained and self-sufficient rural village of a few decades ago. Rapid social change has polarized man's place of residence and his place of work, so that a church that takes its form from the shape of man's dormitory becomes an isolated enclave that is not only racially and socially segregated but has lost touch with the expanding spheres of existence. In his books, *The Suburban Captivity of the Churches* and *The New Creation as Metropolis*, Gibson Winter presents a profound analysis of the problem. Today 63 percent of our population live in "standard metropolitan areas," which are organized on the basis of two principles: functional interdependence and communal insulation. The distinctive features of the first of these principles are the human skills needed in the complex web of the metropolitan economic structure and the impersonality that characterizes the mobilization of these skills. In contrast to the impersonal web of interdependence is the communal insulation of man's place of residence, where "a pattern of segregated communities of personal association shapes the neighborhoods of the metropolis; skin color, style of life, manners and even religious ties create autonomous ghettos of people from a similar occupational level and ethnic background."[18] While one can understand man's drive to protect himself against the threats of impersonality by insulating his residential community against contacts with persons of divergent race or class, the church that becomes aligned with the homogeneous and racially segregated neighborhoods largely renders itself captive to an exclusive sphere of life.

> The residential community in which most pastorates are exercised is no longer the dynamic center of society. Home is the place for licking one's wounds, finding refuge in personal relationships and enjoying a certain leisure. Residence and family life *react to* the dynamics of society, suffering anxieties that are engendered in the productive process. Moreover, the strains of industrial

17. Bender, "Mennonite Conception," 90.
18. Winter, *Suburban Captivity*, 22.

production are such that pastors deal with widespread emotional disturbance in these residential communities without access to the sources of these disturbances. They deal with the symptoms: broken homes, disturbed personalities and delinquent children. The load of personal, pastoral care increases day by day, but the forces that create these problems become daily more remote from the pastor in the residential community. The pastor ministers in a sanitarium, treating the shock cases but never discovering the enemy who is inflicting the damage.

The institutional crisis of Christianity arises, thus, from the preoccupation of the religious community with private concerns while the forces that are shaping human destiny dominate the public realm. Pastors feel this estrangement in their own isolation from the processes of the society—their sense of working in a hothouse atmosphere of women's emotional difficulties and children's programs. Laity experience this crisis in a search for a significant ministry in place of the organizational activities to which the churches usually consign their efforts. Religious leaders sense the depth of this crisis at the very moment when they press for organizational expansion, since the proliferation of residential churches seems to have so little impact on the increasing chaos of the metropolitan areas. The institutional crisis of contemporary Christianity is manifest in the simultaneous appearance of spiritual emptiness and intense religious activity.[19]

The Quest for Remedies

When we move from the current formulations of the indictment against the church to the more constructive parts of the arguments, we can't help but be impressed by the variety of solutions that are proposed and disappointed by much of the discussion on new forms of the church. Idyllic images of new forms are being conceived, but few are the models that seem to point the way. Gibson Winter points to such "foretastes" as lay academies, the small group movement, and "the field of personal, pastoral care,"[20] but he fails totally to specify what it is in these renewal movements that is constitutive of the true church. It is quite possible, nonetheless, to discern and label some of the main lines which the more constructive quest is taking. Three such approaches will be discussed in the paragraphs to follow.

19. Winter, *New Creation*, 29.
20. Winter, *New Creation*, 85–86.

One approach might well be described as "rugged individualism" as an alternative to the irrelevance of the local congregation. The term is actually used by Berger and the editor of *Renewal*,[21] although not as a label for their own positions. To Berger it means, at the very least, that "He who would freely encounter truth must pay the price of being alone," a price that "seems exceptionally high for Americans, who are indoctrinated in an ideology of 'togetherness' practically from infancy."[22] There is a strong Anabaptist ingredient in this affirmation, with its accent on "the decisive turning point that occurs in a human life as a result of encountering the message of Jesus Christ."[23] Berger's disillusionment with the local congregation is so severe, however, that he despairs for its renewal, since it has too many vested interests institutionally, denominationally, culturally, financially, and in every other way to be able to shake loose in any significant way. For this reason, his prescription calls for a large degree of disengagement from the local congregation per se.

> Let there be no uncertainty as to what we are saying: we are suggesting that Christians may freely choose not to become members of local congregations, not to identify themselves with a denomination, not to join the weekly traffic jam of the religious rush hour on Sunday morning. We are suggesting that these decisions might be directly grounded in the Christian faith as it seeks to relate itself to our situation. And we are contending that such decisions might be the legitimate exercise of a Christian vocation in our time.[24]

A delightful critique of this excerpt was given by Robert McAfee Brown in his review of the book in *Union Seminary Quarterly Review*. Brown tried to imagine what the sociological result of Berger's position would be in the lives of the college students for whom he was writing, and his guess was that many would find his solution too easy rather than too demanding:

> *Berger Reader* (having finished page 180 and shut *The Noise of Solemn Assemblies*): Well, thank goodness! I'm off the hook as far as the "church" is concerned. I can be a Christian without being a churchman at all. Let those silly people keep on with their rituals and hymns and communion services and helping individuals

---

21. Berger, *Noise*, 49; Berger, "Whence the Rugged," 9.
22. Berger, *Noise*, 120.
23. Berger, *Noise*, 114.
24. Berger, *Noise*, 177.

in need if they want to. I 'm beyond all that. Now that I see how anachronistic it all is, I'm free.

Instead of that I'll . . . I'll . . . Let's see now, what shall I do? The church can't really change the structures of society and it hasn't got much of a future erecting signs of "Christian presence." I'll have to get into Christian dialogue. But where and how? There isn't any structure around to foster it, and besides, I don't really know the score on the Christian faith. I'll just have to go it alone. But no matter. How nice, how very nice, not to have to feel guilty about the church anymore.[25]

This whimsical critique is squarely to the point. With all of their stress on personal commitment, it can be said to the everlasting credit of the Anabaptists that they also possessed a tenable doctrine of the church. Applying the principle of voluntarism to the matter of structure, they took their task in hand and proceeded to establish the one holy catholic apostolic church. I am often reminded of the words of a professor at Northwestern University in a penetrating essay on the nature of organization. "We may conceive of man as always operating within many sets of limits, and these exist because they are the necessary prices of using the tools of human behavior. If we choose to use the axe, we must heft the burden and if we use people, we must accept their nature as recalcitrant tools, limiting and defining our effectiveness."[26] With all the terrible risks involved in forming a committed, disciplined church of disciples, the Anabaptists did not shrink from the constraints of organization. The theological and practical problem which Berger's books leave almost totally unresolved is the issue of the church. It would not be fair to say that he has no doctrine of the church. He affirms that "when we speak of the task of disestablishment we are not suggesting some sort of social disaffiliation."[27] Nor is he identifying the church in purely mystical terms (his favorite word in this connection is "ecstasy"). One image of new forms which he recommends is that of "ecumenical parish," a supra-parochial association of Christians in a metropolitan area quite similar to the concept that Gibson Winter calls "sector strategy"—the staking out of an area of Christian responsibility across denominational lines from the outer edge of the city to the heart of the inner city along a major line of access or freeway, such an area constituting

---

25. Brown, "Two Books," 339.
26. Greer, *Social Organization*, 10.
27. Berger, *Noise*, 157.

the basic unit for the religious organization of the church's ministry.[28] The concern that we would have is what he does (or rather leaves undone) about the local congregation. After asserting that "the most urgent tasks before us can be dealt with outside the institution and, at least in certain cases, with little reference to it" he concludes:

> The local congregation can then be left to what it has always done and perhaps will always do in the future—liturgy, preaching, the administration of the sacraments, and whatever educational activities seem plausible to those concerned. Essential tasks of the Christian mission in our society can then be undertaken (radically, if need be) outside the local congregation.
>
> Such a conclusion may sound a little like an injunction to let the dead bury their dead. This is not our intention. One might even raise the question of whether some of those who would radically transform the local congregation are quite fair to many in it. For example, there are many of the aged and the sick and the emotionally crippled in our congregations to whom these radical calls for institutional revolution can mean nothing but a threat to whatever spiritual solace the congregation has been able to give them.[29]

Certainly, such a pluralistic conception of Christian response and performance will not commend itself to those of us who reject on theological grounds a hierarchy of callings in the doctrine of Christian vocation. And even if we accepted such a pluralism, we would still need to ask about that half of the church which is not identified with the local congregation. The question as to how a church can be structured to be supra-parochial was not adequately treated by Berger.

A second approach to the problem of the local congregation might best be termed "renewal," apart from the "rugged individualism" we have just discussed and what will next be called "re-formation." The "renewal" approach focuses major attention on the local congregation. The very word, "renewal," implies that the churches now in existence can be revived and restored. This approach to church renewal does not really meddle with traditional issues of faith and order. Its main concern is with expanding the work of the church in the world rather than altering the prior framework of the established church as a societal institution, except that the corollary of expansion in the secular realm is a de-emphasis of concentration

---

28. Winter, *Suburban Captivity*, 171.
29. Berger, *Noise*, 170.

on intra-church program, equipment, and buildings. Gibson Winter's latest book, *The New Creation as Metropolis*, certainly falls into this category, with its view of metropolis as the brotherhood of the future, the image of Christianity as the servanthood of the laity within the structures of metropolis, and the work of the professional ministry as auxiliary to the work of the laity. This is also the editorial approach of *Renewal* magazine, published by the Chicago City Missionary Society and "devoted to the renewal of the Church in the metropolis." Copy for the December 1963 issue was prepared entirely by the editor, Stephen C. Rose, and sets out to present "A Positive Program" for the renewal of the local congregation:

> In the context of the need to streamline the local church program and free the minister from the burden of administration, the following steps might be taken:
>
> Churches with multiple staffs should hire laymen to handle administrative tasks such as fundraising, building maintenance, etc. When an individual congregation cannot afford this, such services should be obtained cooperatively with other churches. Ministers should be free to do what they were trained to do: prepare sermons, make pastoral calls, and become "chaplains to the laity."
>
> Unless absolutely necessary, church construction should be limited to cooperative ventures on the part of several churches. There is no good reason why Christian education in a given community cannot take place in a central facility available to all Protestant groups. Duplication of facilities wastes time, money, and effort. Directors of Christian education hired by several churches should pool their resources to form a cooperative faculty, conducting classes throughout the week rather than confining the main emphasis to the often awkward Sunday School hour. Whenever possible, curriculum for Christian education should be developed on the local level so that national denominations can begin to cut down on the enormous expense of producing materials that are often useless at the local level.
>
> Most lay activities within the church should be carefully re-evaluated and redirected. Service to the community should be the criterion and there should be absolutely no barriers to service once needs are determined. If the major community problem is divorce, let the local church meet that problem, perhaps using the church building as a marriage-counselling clinic. The church building should be open to the community at all times. In communities where people are lonely and in need of friendship, perhaps the greatest service the local congregation can render is

to keep the doors open and the coffee pot on, providing a place where people feel free to come, sit, talk, meet others. Groups like Gamblers Anonymous, Alcoholics Anonymous, peace movements, and other worthwhile efforts should be free to use the church's physical plant.

Local congregations should conduct an ongoing study of denominational programs and expenses, and adjust their contributions to denominations on bases like the following: How much money is going into service? Is the denomination trying to work cooperatively with other denominations? It may be that local programs, in which laymen are actively involved, are more worthy of direct support.

Fundraising should be limited to a single annual appeal, preferably a pledge system. Special offerings should be limited or eliminated, and all fundraising activities of church organizations should be drastically curtailed: fairs, bazaars, bake sales, etc.

The local church should not regard Sunday morning as the only time during the week for public worship. Hours of public worship should be determined by the needs of the community. All Protestant churches should offer Holy Communion on a weekly basis or perhaps twice weekly so that all members may have the opportunity to share the sacrament.

Churches should re-evaluate the meaning of membership, requiring in-depth training for new members and courses for old members who have not had training. Basic education for membership should include an introduction to the Old and New Testament, a course in church history, a course in contemporary social problems from the Christian perspective, and special-interest courses designed to equip members for service in the world.[30]

Certainly we can second many or most of the above recommendations for the renewal of the local congregation, but the fact remains that, like Gibson Winter's new metropolis, Rose does not specify what it is in these suggestions that is constitutive of the authentic church, since he decided in advance not to interfere with the basic order of ecclesiastical affairs, from which the practices which he wants to alter are derived.

The third type of approach to the problem of the church may be called "reformation" in distinction to "renewal." The label as well as the approach is developed by Gordon Cosby of the Church of the Saviour in Washington. In an article entitled "Not Renewal, but Reformation," Cosby writes, "When the structures get as rigid and as resistant to change as they are now,

---

30. Rose "Positive Program," 10–11.

perhaps the wisest strategy is not to try to renew them. It may be a wiser strategy to bypass them and let God do with them what He will. The new structures which will appear may be so drastically different from the old as to constitute reform rather than renewal."[31]

Cosby's thesis is that the shape of the church grows out of its mission: He is convinced that "the structures in which the church is at present contained are irrelevant and simply do not allow the church to be on mission. They hinder the proclamation of the gospel rather than further it."[32] Although Cosby does not hesitate to suggest what he thinks the new structures of the church may look like, he believes that no one can know in advance what forms God will bring into being for particular times and situations. "The strategy, the tactics of the church, the shape, the patterns, the structures in which it will express itself are all determined as a result of obedience to the living God. God leads His people day by day, moment by moment."[33] He believes further that no pattern can be absolutized for all time. Since the pattern is subservient to mission, an important clue in this approach is that "the shape of the church will be determined in large measure by the world,"[34] even as the world in large measure determined the shape of our Lord's ministry, including the form of his death. Cosby presents the following possibilities for serious consideration:

> I think we ought to be open to the giving up of all professional ministries. It may be that I ought to earn my livelihood another way. Perhaps all of the ministers of a congregation should be engaged in a tent-making ministry and do their job in the life of the world.
>
> Another possibility is that of giving up all real estate. I think our present real estate serves us, but I think that a pilgrim people ought always to be open to the possibility of giving up all its real estate. If the bomb were to fall on this area, we would have to be the church without any real estate. The church was the church during the most vibrant period of its life, several hundred years, without real estate.
>
> Another possibility is that the church might carry out its mission through small bands of people, just two or three or four or five, who would live out their lives in the midst of the world of business,

---

31. Cosby, "Not Renewal," 4.
32. Cosby, "Not Renewal," 4.
33. Cosby, "Not Renewal," 4.
34. Cosby, "Not Renewal," 5.

the world of government, the world of mass media, the medical world, the educational world—out there where they are making their tents, earning their living. Such little mission groups would be working at the problems of mass media, or on the issues relating to peace and prevention of war, or on race relations and housing, or with the poor, perhaps taking a vow of poverty.

I am not talking about little functional groups related to the local congregation. These mission groups of which I speak would be the local congregation. We need to redefine the meaning of congregation. "Where two or three are gathered together in my name, there am I in the midst of them." This is the beginning point.

What does it mean to gather—to "congregate"—in the name of Christ? It means to have been baptized into His nature. To have died with Him and risen with Him. It presupposes commitment. The congregation is a people to whom the Word of God is preached and to whom the sacraments are administered. These things do not have to be done by a professional minister; anyone who is appointed by that community of faith may do them.[35]

I have followed the development of the Church of the Saviour since its beginning in 1947 and have always been deeply impressed by its high standards of membership, its objective discipline, its exceptional stewardship of money and talents, its stress on evangelism, its rigorous program of Christian education, and its corporate ministries to the desperate needs of its community.[36] In two ways in particular, it provides us with a model for the reformation of the twentieth century church. First, in relation to locus or territoriality, it is not structured as a parish or residence church in the traditional sense of operating within a defined geographical area for the total population. Its constitutive principle is the structured discipleship of its members without basic regard to geography. Second, in relation to money and equipment, it has never been a "mission church" in the traditional sense of receiving subsidies from sources outside of itself nor of relying heavily on building or equipment for its program. It began on an indigenous, self-supporting, self-propagating basis from the beginning. It does have a headquarters, which is an old three-story house; but the fact that a new highway is to be built through the land on which this property stands presents no serious threat to the continuation of this church.

---

35. Cosby, "Not Renewal," 5–6.
36. See O'Connor, *Call to Commitment*.

Anyone who joins the ranks of the dissidents who are seeking new forms of the church and her ministry risks considerable presumption at numerous points. One point is the level of personal commitment and obedience. Walter Wagoner exposes this point of vulnerability when he suggests that much talk about the irrelevance of old forms may be "a mere stalling tactic by which not angry but frightened young men refuse the call to Macedonia," a way by which "sophisticated verbosity" becomes but another "form of apostasy."[37] Another point is the level of theological maturity and cogency. We have already noted that the remedial category described by the caption, "rugged individualism," leaves unresolved the issue of the church as integral to the gospel. The "renewal of the church" approach deals largely with symptoms of ecclesiastical disorder rather than with causes and leaves the basic issues of faith and order unmolested. The "reformation" approach is at once the most original and transformational of the types of remedies discussed; but it could turn out that the only difference between "renewal" and "reformation" is the matter of time. Those who disavow the old structures and set out to create new ones will have ultimately to face the very same pressures that corrupted the old ones. When seen in its biblical perspective, the theme of renewal embraces reformation, for it has to do with an ongoing confrontation between God and man in his corporate and individual life in covenant context. It is particularly presumptuous to deny what evidences there be that God is at work in existing churches as though his only option were to bring in a decisively new solution at this moment in history.

Marks of the Church's Authenticity

Evasion or neutrality, on the other hand, are dubious virtues in the face of the current indictments against the church; and one of our greatest needs is the willingness to search constantly for authenticity in the Christian enterprise. The search for authenticity, of course, implies a basis of authority. Some will turn to the Bible as the ground of authority for the norms of the church. Others will turn to some historical stance, especially one that has produced a rich heritage for its heirs along a particular tributary in the rivers of time. Others will affirm the needs of the hour and employ a functional criterion in their doctrine of the church. While these do not exhaust the possibilities, they indicate that we have to reckon with the way we come to these topics

---

37. Wagoner, *Bachelor of Divinity*, 65.

with our own presuppositions, whether hidden or exposed. I will admit, therefore, that the following attempt to specify the marks of authenticity in the church derives from an Anabaptist point of view and may provide at least some criteria for judging the historical authenticity of what is being done by those who claim to stand in this Reformation tradition:

1. *A binding fellowship.* A fellowship in the gospel in which binding decisions are made by the leading of the Holy Spirit to carry out the mandates Christ has laid upon his church.

2. *Discipleship.* A membership based on a voluntary and accountable pledge of each person to obey Christ in thoroughgoing discipleship and to listen continually for the next Word from the Lord, thus bringing one's whole existence under a radical lordship of Christ.

3. *Discipline.* A corporate and objective discipline by which all members are girded for their ministries and by which faltering or unwilling members are restored or in exceptional cases excluded.

4. *Evangelism.* A moving back and forth between church and world, bringing converts along into the fellowship, where the Christian way is practiced in every relationship of life.

5. *Nurture in the church.* A ministry of upbuilding and nurture within the congregation, including such functions as Bible teaching, counseling, regulation of the group life, and the instruction and evangelism of the children.

6. *Servanthood in the world.* A ministry of proclamation and servanthood to the world, taking the form of missions to areas of human need by smaller or larger task forces from within the congregation.

7. *Leadership.* The wide distribution of leadership responsibility in the carrying out of these ministries and missions, having no formal or impersonal distinctions (e.g., clergy, laity).

8. *Stewardship.* The financing of these ministries and the meeting of all human need through the sharing of money and possessions.

9. *Worship.* The regular corporate retreat for worship in modes which are indigenous to the local congregation and led by the servants of the group life.

10. *Love and nonresistance.* The application of the teachings of Christ, particularly the all-embracing ethic of love and nonresistance, in every situation of life.

I suspect that any attempt to specify the marks of authenticity in the church in propositional terms such as the above can never meet with total approval. To be specific one might anticipate a number of areas of ambiguity in which we might hope for clearer light to break in upon us in the months to come.

Remaining Ambiguities

One of these has to do with the church as means and end. A major theme of much of the current literature on church renewal is a new emphasis on mission as central to the true nature of the church, and often the emphasis is made by asserting that "the church is mission." While one can try to understand what it means to say that mission belongs to the essential being of the church, it is probably truer to the meaning of the church to say that the church is more than just a means to make the gospel known to the world; it is part of the gospel and thus is end as well as means. The danger in the way the new stress on mission is put is to assign to the church a position subordinate to other aspects of the gospel. Christ founded the church not only to send it out into the world to preach and serve but to introduce alongside of the world a new and transforming kind of community. The very existence of the church as an end in itself is a witness to the world of that which God has done, is doing, and will yet do.

This is not to say, however, that the Great Commission can be fulfilled by simply "being the church," as the case of the Hutterites shows so well. Unless a congregation is involved in missions to the areas of need round about, its own vitality will likely diminish and die. And as history shows all too well, it will likely be involved in missions only when it is so structured that a missionary encounter in the world becomes deliberate, planned, and objective. The paradox of the church in history as both end and means is something like the rising and receding of a tide. At times the instrumental dimension recedes far into the background. At other times it rises in importance, at last rushing in upon the minds of Christians with such force that it constitutes a new revelation in itself. Clearly the age of world missions by proxy is ending, and each church now has a missionary task for its own environment. The urgency that lies in back of this conviction is not only the belief that the church has a mission to perform in the world (i.e., means) but that it can only know its true existence as an end in itself through the act of carrying out that mission in the same way that some depths of the mystery of what it means to be a Christian can only come to us in the act of winning others to our Lord and to his way.

Related to this ambiguity is another which has to do with the categories of church and world. Most of the current attempts to describe the church in terms of its role as a servant of God's mission to the world dissolve the boundary lines between church and world. Because of this, the theology of the relationship between church and world needs careful examination. A view of the church as merely a piece of the world which confesses Christ will tend to undercut the valuation of the church as a part of the gospel and probably also to undermine the ethical discipline of the church, for if we are to assume that church and world are mere parts of one great harmonious whole, there will likely be no significant difference between life in the church and life in the world. A view of the church and world as separate and disharmonious realms will mean a substantial difference not only to the nature of the church-world dialogue but also to the nature of the intra-church dialogue. The marks which distinguish the church from the world may become signs to the world of God's purpose for the world, and the life within the church will then need to be such that these signs are clearly evident.

Again, however, this is not to say that the arbitrary way the line between church and world has been drawn in traditional Mennonite circles can ever be authenticated by cultural geographical norms. This line is ever precarious and certainly more dynamic than the traditional demarcation would suggest. All that can be said, perhaps, is that the line will have to be reinterpreted and redrawn, in order to enliven, rather than to quench, the church's mission to the world. Since "the wind blows where it wills" we can never accept a spatial separation between church and world. Our problem is that we have so little experience in our generation to suggest what it would mean to say that "separation from the world" is a spiritual rather than a spatial matter.

A third ambiguity related to the other two has to do with the Christian's vocation within the structures of the world. The notion found in much of the current literature on church renewal that the Christian ministry of a servant church is the work of laity in the world with an undergirding from theological specialists is at least a misinterpretation of the New Testament materials concerning ministry. References to the diversity of ministries in the New Testament (Rom 12, 1 Cor 12) identify these gifts with functions appropriate to the life and work of a congregation and not to functions in secular society. Yet, to say that a Christian's only ministry is within the structure of the congregation tends to obscure the truth that the church is in the world even though its identity remains distinct. In a world in which all men are interdependent and in which Christians will always be working alongside non-Christians in the economic realm, it is misleading to differentiate sharply between "church vocations" and "secular vocations" for the Christian. If we conceive of the church as the matrix for the totality of the Christian's life, even though he is economically interdependent with non-Christians, then one vocation (e.g., evangelist) is no more distinctly a church vocation than another (e.g., tentmaking). As a matter of Paul's own experience, the Christian who has the gifts of an evangelist might at the same time be gainfully employed as a tentmaker, which indicates that one of the important ways in which all Christians are Christian is through their occupations, whatever that might be by the leading of God. Only with such a dynamic conception of Christian vocation can we then begin to talk about certain Christians who are set apart for special assignments needing seminary training, some to be salaried by the church, and others to be carried out on a self-supporting basis. For all believers, however, the congregation remains the primary context for the living of one's life; and whatever any believer does should carry the call and sanction of the brethren.

A fourth ambiguity has to do with the essence-form relationship in our doctrine of the church. What is the relationship of our partnership in the gospel to the structures which inevitably spring from it? In his study of the changing forms of the church's witness, Colin Williams recalls Wesley's distinction between "instituted" and "prudential" means of grace, the former referring to those instituted by Christ as unchangeable characteristics of the church—such as prayer, searching the Scriptures, the sacraments, fasting, and waiting—and the latter referring to the changing structures of the Christian life required to relate it to the changing situations in which Christians find themselves.

> Wesley saw his own "societies" as an expression of prudential means of grace which he struggled to keep within the Church of England, believing that in the life of the church the continuity of the "instituted" means of grace was given. But he believed that his societies were vital to the mission of the church because they provided for the necessary "prudential" forms in which the changeless

life of the church could be brought to men in the changing circumstances of their life.[38]

This distinction between "instituted" and "prudential" means of grace is helpful as we grapple with the essence-form problem. It would warn us, on one hand, "against any restructuring which threatens to jettison those means of grace given to the church by Christ as permanent and essential characteristics of her life." But it would also warn us against forgetting "that the church must always develop forms of life which will provide the ways by which these 'means of grace' may produce a Christian style of life as the believers participate in the particular structures of the life of their own age."[39]

A fifth ambiguity has to do with whether forms are derivative from, rather than constitutive of, the essence of the church. By asserting that forms are changeable, we do not mean that they are optional; and we have still to ask, then, whether and to what extent the structure of the church is a constitutive principle of the church. We may speak, for example, of the "local congregation" as a given constitutive form of the church; but the fact is that some of the principal writers about church renewal today are seriously questioning the legitimacy of the empirical church precisely at the point of the local congregation. The crux of the question probably focuses on the meaning of the term "local." If by "local" we mean that the identity of the congregation is residential or geographical (e.g., the parish church) or historical or cultural (e.g., the denominational church) or dogmatic (e.g., the fundamentalist church), we might readily agree that these forms are not constitutive of the church, even though they continue to be the predominant organizational principles by which most local congregations are established. If by "local" we mean that the identity of the congregation is a group of people who interact with each other as whole personalities, sharing the totality of their lives in obedience to Jesus Christ, then we might well say that "congregationalism" is a given characteristic of the church.

New Forms of the Congregation

This brings us to the vital question: What are the forms that will help to make the church authentic for such a time as this? Although we should expect to designate these forms, whatever they may be, as "local

---

38. Williams, *Where in the World*, 62.
39. Williams, *Where in the World*, 62–63.

congregations" in the meaning that was given at the end of the preceding section, a strong case can be made against the conclusion that the residential congregation, which has been normative for over one thousand years, is necessarily the best structure for the church in our day. Colin Williams, who gives perhaps the most convincing argument against the residential congregation as normative for our time, develops the provocative thesis that the structures of the congregation should bear a direct relationship to the structures of the world in her need.[40] According to this proposition, the staff and patients of Oaklawn Psychiatric Center could constitute a Christian congregation in every sense of the term, provided it met certain theological requirements, i.e., incorporated the "instituted" means of grace. This, then, would be an example of a congregation structured around a conspicuous need of the world. It is in this sense that the Church of the Saviour in Washington is now beginning to refer to the satellite congregations within its orbit—the Renewal Center Congregation, the Rockville House Congregation, and the Congregation of the Potter's House, the latter being a coffee house where artists and writers, businessmen and scientists, poets and beatniks, gather to discuss issues of Christian concern. This concept of satellite congregations grew out of the experience of trying to meet the needs of the particular situation, as the following excerpt from the history of the Church of the Saviour reveals:

> We look at the structure which is the Potter's House and wonder what are its frontiers. One night last month a minister who had left the church to take a job in the State Department talked to us excitedly about the coffee house. He said, "This is what I knew the church should be and I didn't know how to go about it. I want to attend your church." We invited him to worship with us on a Sunday morning and he came eager and open, but the traditional church service in our blue chapel disappointed him, and he said in effect, "I'll stick to the Potter's House." There crossed our minds the thought that perhaps on Sunday mornings there should be a worship service at the Potter's House and that out of this congregation might grow a liturgy suitable not only for the market place, but a liturgy expressing the generation of abstract paintings and modern technology and space travel—a generation who may need their own setting to discover the majestic grandeur of cathedrals

---

40. Williams, *Where in the World*, 59, 69, 70, 75.

and the simple loveliness of blue chapels, the friendship of St. Francis, of Brother Lawrence, and of Bonhoeffer.[41]

It has been argued that a congregation like this is not a true congregation because it does not minister to the whole people of God—men and women and children of all ages—but only to a small segment of society and a restricted age group. But as Colin Williams points out, "If that criterion is used, where is there a true congregation? Our local communities are now usually a highly restricted section—a particular class, color, language, cultural group; and related only to the residential aspect of the lives of that particular group. If the criterion should be that a congregation must represent the whole people of God, that it should reveal the manner in which the life of Christ transcends the barriers of age, of race, of nation, of class, of language; then the present local congregation singularly fails to meet the test."[42] The accepted assumption that the residence congregation is the normative form of church life is nothing less than "morphological fundamentalism."[43] It is only one option, although we might add an important option, inasmuch as human domicile is, and will probably be for a long time to come, one important structure of the needs of the world. But there are other structures which could be just as legitimate bases for the formation of Christian congregations as that of residence. Some of the alternative structures of the world as bases for Christian congregation are catalogued by Colin Williams as follows:

1. *Direct sociological structures* giving rise to continuing institutions—such as political structures, business, vocational groups, communications and entertainment media, educational and health institutions.

2. *Communities of concern* (e.g., the "world" of the arts) and communities of need (e.g., drug addicts). Unlike the first group these are not so much organized institutions as changing communities gathering around the concerns and needs.

3. *Major social crises* necessitating structured responses—e.g., race, housing, poverty, war.[44]

---

41. O'Connor, *Call to Commitment*, 187.
42. Williams, *Where in the World*, 9–10.
43. Williams, *Where in the World*, 11.
44. Williams, *Where in the World*, 84.

In short, a congregation can be defined as "any gathering of Christians which is called by Christ to witness to his lordship in particular areas of the world's life; and that just as this can occur in residence, so it also can occur in other 'worlds.'"[45]

We turn, now, to the question of new forms for Mennonite congregationalism. How can the congregation be so structured that it will achieve the historic intentions of faith and ethics as interpreted by the Mennonites? In order to discuss this question in proper perspective, we should be clear about one thing. The Holy Spirit is still at work in the Mennonite rural community church which H. S. Bender described as "the brotherhood of love in which all the members minister to each other in all their needs both temporal and spiritual."[46] This is the old structure that most of us grew up in and in which we came to know Jesus Christ. Agriculture will continue to be one important structure of the world around which Christian congregations must take form. But we simply have to face with more courage than we have shown so far that in a large-scale affluent society, less than 5 percent of the population will raise the food and fiber for the rest of the population. Already in our generation, the majority of Mennonites no longer belong to Mennonite rural community churches in the sense in which Harold Bender was speaking; but we have been reluctant to allow the full impact of this fact to enter into our thinking and planning.

With insight and boldness, J. Lawrence Burkholder has confronted the facts of rapid social change and faced the question of Mennonitism for tomorrow. In his *Christian Century* article in the "What's Ahead for the Churches?" series, he states his belief that "the greatest contribution that the peace churches can make to Christendom lies in the area of the concept of the congregation."[47] It is his belief, moreover, that this contribution ought to be made in the form of experimental models as signs to the other churches and to the world that the Lord does have a word to speak to the present and oncoming generation. The particular dimension of the congregational life which he projects into these future experimental models is that of ethical discernment—the structuring of the congregation as an ethical community, making ethical decisions and implementing them in the world. "The crux of the matter," he feels, "is

---

45. Williams, *Where in the World*, 97.
46. Bender, "Mennonite Conception," 90.
47. Burkholder, "Peace Churches," 1072.

the decision-making process."⁴⁸ The congregation of the future has got to be re-formed so that the adult Sunday school classes and congregational meetings become more than mere forums for the exchange of ideas, but can become springboards to binding decisions about such great issues as war, race, housing, capital punishment, unemployment, and poverty. "Congregations restructured as discerning communities would concertedly seek to meet specific needs in the world" and they "would be ordered around works of love in lowly places."⁴⁹

> Its identity would be established by what it "does" in a local situation in the world. Worship, fellowship, sacraments, teaching, and discipline would belong to the life of the congregation, but these would not be detached from specific ministries. To the outsider such a congregation would look more like a local Peace Corps unit or a closely related set of such units than a band of worshipers. The church building would reflect the modesty of faith rather than the imperial character of Christendom. It would be a headquarters for a number of missions or "task forces," each such entity operating essentially as the church, i.e., as a serving, worshiping, disciplining fellowship. The congregation would thus be primarily an assembly of mission fellowships, not an assembly of individuals. Membership would depend largely on willingness to pay the price of radical discipleship. Not everyone would join such a church, but the basis for exclusion would be preferable to that which is now used in many "inclusive" churches.⁵⁰

Although the structural details which Burkholder describes as part of his vision of the ethically discerning congregation raise many and provocative questions, there is one facet which he discusses which is undebatable and squarely to the point. Whatever form the church takes within a period of history, the crucial problem is to discern what the Lord would say to us in the congregation about the needs of the world round about, the needs of the brethren within the church for worship, education, and dialogue, and the gifts within the church to meet these needs within and without. "If Christ does not become a living reality within the congregation, then it would appear misleading to discuss problems that presume that He has. Better admit quite frankly that the peace churches are not

---

48. Burkholder, "Peace Churches," 1073.
49. Burkholder, "Peace Churches," 1073.
50. Burkholder, "Peace Churches," 1074.

certain about what constitutes obedience today and that Christian ethics in the deepest sense does not exist among them."[51]

I turn, finally, to a vision which all of this talk about church renewal and reformation has conjured up in the mind of the writer. I think we have to admit that we can't possibly perceive all of the possibilities of renewal and reformation within our own conferences and congregations. This can become a strong temptation simply to write them off as visionary, impractical, unrealistic. In my mind there is no doubt that the majority of our local congregations are vulnerable to the indictments that were discussed above: many have become establishments of a cultural continuity; some have been victimized by the values of middle-class business ethics; and most are captive to the sphere of residence. Unlike Peter Berger, who believes that individualism is the best alternative to an irrelevant church, or Gordon Cosby, who believes that the wisest strategy is to bypass the existing structures in favor of new ones, I believe that the Holy Spirit is still at work in the old structures. There is substantial evidence that many members of established congregations are far more ready to obey the promptings of the living Spirit of Christ than we usually suppose, when there arises in their midst a servant leader who is prepared, through total identification and suffering with his people, to introduce them to the living Spirit. I know that this is happening in numerous congregations across our conference.

One of the problems is that these evidences of new life are so quickly extinguished or minimized because they appear piecemeal on the local level and they are not tied in with the experimentations of other congregations out of which a cumulation of evidence of the working of the Holy Spirit could provide an important ingredient that is missing: corroboration.

This is where conference boards and committees ought to come into the picture, with two types of ministries. One of these is to confirm the genuine fruits of the gospel ministry in a local congregation by the simple input of accounts of similar workings of the Spirit in sister congregations. This is the experience of corroboration which has a dynamic consolidating effect upon the faithful members of any church, as any conference leader who has been able to fulfill this crucial role can testify. One can hardly imagine or underestimate the leavening influence in our congregations of reports they are now getting about the creative work in Kansas City, or in Winnipeg, or in Atlanta, or in the current Johannestal-Brudertal negotiations in Hillsboro. This is especially the case when these reports support

---

51. Burkholder, "Peace Churches," 1075.

similar stirrings of the Spirit in the widely separated local congregations to which the reports come.

The other ministry is precisely what Burkholder calls "experimental models" or "pilot projects" as signs to the other churches and to the world that the Spirit does bring to our remembrance all that Jesus began to do and to teach. Although I would not reject the possibility that such models could emerge from established churches, I am envisioning projects that would probably begin apart from established churches in order to have the freedom to go beyond the familiar patterns of ministry and in order to shatter the captivity to the domestic sphere of residence. Again, a conference board or committee (and particularly the board of missions and its satellite committees) has an unusual opportunity to implement just such pilot projects of congregational life, for the reason that these agencies can deal with a great variety of concerns that local churches do not have access to. We are doing this in many areas: migrant ministries, psychiatric services, interracial units, voluntary services, etc. For some strange reason, we have done almost nothing of this sort that is essentially centered in the concept of the congregation.

The vision is for a select group of "ministers" to commit themselves for at least half a decade or longer to any new program (urban, rural, interracial, etc.) about which they, together with the sponsoring conference board or committee, would agree should be attempted by the leading of the Holy Spirit. Quite possibly, this pilot congregation would model itself after the shape of some worldly need (employment, education, human blight, prejudice, dereliction, poverty, etc.). Whatever the project might be, provided it incorporates the "instituted means of grace" and is truly relevant to the selected area of worldly need, there would be innumerable individuals in our conference, particularly at our colleges and seminary, who would be delighted to get involved in the extension of this experiment. My guess is that we would be awed by the ramifications of such a project, not the least of which would be a feedback to the established congregations with the suggestion, "Why not try this for size?" That this vision is not completely original with me, although it is certainly a unique possibility for our own tradition, will be evident in the following concluding remark from Walter Wagoner:

> It [some experimental model for a new form of the church and her witness] would be more than a safety valve for steamy impatience; it would be the church's recognition that just as is true of

any university or industry, it must have a department of subsidized revolutions where creative persons can get a hearing within the established structures of church life, without waiting for years to get into a position of authority.[52]

---

52. Wagoner, *Bachelor of Divinity*, 64.

10

The Renewal of the Church

John W. Miller

Part I

When we speak about the renewal of the church we are touching on the problem of a faithless and disobedient church. We are thinking about a church that has lost its way, and we are asking how this church might find its way again. In this sense we might say that the Christian church at the very beginning was a renewal movement within the disobedient church of Israel. It challenged that church to bring forth the deeds of repentance. This being the case, it must seem strange that the Christian church should today be so preoccupied with its own renewal as it seems to be. And we might well ask, did Jesus foresee a development of this kind? Did he realize that even his own movement, so new and vital in its time, would one day grow old and lifeless and itself need renewal? If so, did he leave us any instructions as to what to do in such circumstances?

To both questions we can answer, "Yes." I have long felt that ecumenical Christianity has paid insufficient attention in its discussions of church unity and church renewal to the warnings of Jesus recorded at the conclusion of the Sermon on the Mount. In those warnings Jesus clearly indicates that he had no false optimism about the future of his movement. John says of Jesus that he knew the hearts of men and did not need anyone else to tell him what was in a man. Unlike many a sectarian leader, Jesus saw straight through to the possibilities of corruption in his would-be disciples. "Not everyone who says to me, Lord, Lord, shall enter the kingdom of heaven, but he who does the will of my Father who is in heaven" (Matt 7:21). One of the most fearful things Jesus ever said is contained in a statement that immediately follows this one: "On that day many will say to me, Lord, Lord, did we not prophesy in your name, and cast out demons in your name, and do many mighty works in your name? And then will I declare to them, I never knew you; depart from me, you evildoers" (Matt 7:22–23). And then Jesus goes on to distinguish, with unmistakable simplicity, two types of churches, two types of houses, houses built on rock and houses built on sand. And what distinguishes them is that in one instance there is hearing and doing, and in the other hearing only.

Jesus, then, did clearly anticipate the problem of faithlessness within his own following. On down through the ages, these statements seem to imply, there will be many who take the name of Jesus in a hypocritical way. There will be a false church, in which Jesus is worshiped, in which prophesying goes on in his name, in which even miracles of healing take place, but in which there is no good fruit, in which the words of Jesus are not obeyed. And there will be a faithful church, a church that follows Jesus in simple obedience and does the will of the heavenly Father. This situation Jesus saw clearly, and consequently the apostasy of many of his followers came as no bitter disillusionment to him.

This may seem a rather dark point to make at the very outset of a discussion of the renewal of the church. But we must become quite sober and realistic about the church. The church is not all one thing. Jesus saw that his following would be a mixed multitude, a conglomerate of disobedience and obedience, full of the same kind of hypocrisy that he so roundly condemned in the Jewish church of his own time.

This is a side of things which I fear the ecumenical movement has not sufficiently grasped. The ecumenical movement has done a great service in helping many Christians see that the lines between the true and the false church do not run along the established denominational lines. It has helped us acknowledge the increasing meaninglessness of these artificial bodies. At the same time, it has created an atmosphere of tolerance that tones down our genuine horror for the evil perpetuated by the churches. It has blinded us to the fact that many churches which make a very orthodox confession of Jesus are not true churches at all, if measured by obedience to his words. It is only a rare, courageous soul who will break the tranquility and self-congratulatory atmosphere in which the churches live in this ecumenical era, with words like the following taken from a letter received from Clarence Jordan:

> For years (Clarence writes) I have proclaimed . . . that the church is the realm of redemption. But during the past few years it has been dawning on me that what we call churches are not churches at all, and to naively expect them to rise up and respond to the gospel is, to say the least, unintelligent. The average church member is about as serious about the lordship of Jesus Christ as the average Klan member is. By and large, churches have so repudiated their Head, and so identified with the world that the only thing they retain of their former Spouse is His name, which they take in vain. I know this sounds bitter and cynical, but it is based on firsthand, intimate contact over many years, and I believe it is a factual statement rather than a bitter opinion. I think that there was far more hope for the pharisaism of Jesus's day than for the ecclesiasticism of our day.

Most of us find words like these harsh, but they are no harsher than the words of Jesus himself as he projects the future of his movement.

If this is the situation of the church, we might well cry out in despair. How then will the church ever be renewed? The fact is that Jesus does not anticipate the kind of renewal that many in our time seem to anticipate. Unless I am mistaken, he does not even speak of renewal. Instead he speaks of something about which none of us wishes to speak—judgment! Those churches that persist in saying, "Lord, Lord," while failing to do the will of the heavenly Father, cannot look forward to renewal but to judgment. In our optimistic way we want to think about renewing these disobedient churches. Many earnest Christians today feel torn as to whether they should work in congregations where there is much disobedience and try to renew them or go out on missions into new places. Many make the choice to work with these disobedient congregations. There they may even compromise themselves in order to keep peace with their people. They do not know that even while they are trying to renew these churches, God has already set in motion forces of judgment. "You are the salt of the earth; but if salt has lost its taste, how can its saltness be restored? It is no longer good for anything except to be thrown out and trodden under foot by men." That is the destiny of a disobedient church. There is a condition that cannot be renewed. There are churches that are beyond reformation. To speak about the renewal of such churches is like speaking about re-salting salt.

Instead then of speaking of the renewal of the churches, which may lead us into a false optimism, we must learn from Jesus and the prophets before him to face up to the reality of judgment. If we want to persist in using the word renewal, we might say that God renews the church by judgment. We can see in our own time how the fruitless branches of Christendom are being lopped off and thrown upon the trash heap. The saltless salt is being cast out and trodden under by the foot of men. I am speaking of the purging that has come upon the church in Hitler's Germany, in Communist Russia, and elsewhere in our time. That is God's answer to hypocritical Christianity in history, and on the day of judgment there will be heard the words, "I never knew you."

If then there is a disobedient Christianity that will not be renewed, according to Jesus, but judged, purged, and destroyed, what is there for us to do? The only hope that Jesus holds out for any of us is that in the midst of all this false Christianity, all this hypocrisy, some might have ears to hear and hearts to obey. The hope of Jesus lies in the expectation that somewhere those will gather who have understanding enough, boldness enough, and integrity enough to follow him, not in word only but in deed. All his warnings and urgent admonitions are designed to call this forth, to prick the conscience and challenge the will.

Many people lament the condition of Christianity with its confusing array of movements, sects, and cults. They are looking for a day when there will be one church, one united Christian body. That is not the expectation I get from reading the words of Jesus. There I get a picture of just the kind of confusion I see about me today. But there too I hear a ringing warning to watch out in the midst of this confusion. There I am led to hope in a church that will, in the midst of all the confusion, and in the midst of the judgments of history, stand firm on a solid rock. There I am led to believe that a people can follow Jesus, can live faithfully under his easy yoke, and in so doing will season and light the world.

That is what Jesus leads me to care about, and to care supremely about. I do not know about the renewal of the church. Under the banner of Christianity fearful things have been and are being perpetuated. Under the banner of Christianity wars have been fought, slavery practiced, injustices defended, heretics killed, and much more. Jesus has not sent us to renew all that. He sends us forth as his disciples to "disciple" the nations, teaching them to obey all the things he taught. My uppermost desire in life is to do just that, and my concern in these lectures is to encourage you to do the same.

I would like now to discuss three stumbling-blocks that get in the way of the kind of straightforward obedience to Jesus I am referring to, and then

I want to turn to some specific issues of obedience which I believe have special significance for the church in our time.

I think a complete stranger to our age, looking in on the Christian movement today and then examining those texts which the movement professes to look to as authoritative for its style of life, would shake his head in great perplexity. If someone says, "I am a Marxist," or "I am a Gandhian," we assume that we can go to the teaching and life of Karl Marx or of Gandhi and discover there something about that person. Likewise, if someone says, "I am a Christian," one would think that something could be said about that person by reading in the Gospels about Jesus the Christ. But here an objective observer would discover an absurdity. The church for the most part callously disregards the most central and clear teachings of Jesus on a host of critical issues like war, racial prejudice, and economics and preoccupies itself with a series of activities about which he said nothing. And not only is it a matter of misunderstanding, but in many instances of neglect and disinterest. If Jesus is Lord, one would suppose that every word of his is a command. If he is King of history, one would suppose the Christian church would rather suffer and perish before neglecting one of his standing orders. But the situation is such that even in our seminaries, even among our ministers, not to speak of others, the teaching of Jesus on many matters is disregarded. The market is flooded with books from the great theologians. Students eagerly debate the different philosophical, ethical, and psychological trends of our time, with scarcely a reference to Jesus. His words are no longer marching orders for the Christian movement.

How can we explain such a situation?

(1) I will mention first of all an answer to this question which Jesus himself pointed to again and again: hypocrisy. Beware of the leaven of the Pharisees, Jesus said, which is hypocrisy. And no one who has read the Gospels will ever forget with what stinging irony he exposes the hypocrisy of these respected religious leaders of his time. Hypocrisy has to do with profession without reality. It is the kind of danger into which religious professionals are prone to fall, and when they do, it can become a stumbling-block to many who look to them for leadership. This was the case with the Pharisees. Their own failure to practice what they preached acted as a stumbling-block to many others. It made the common people content to remain at the same level of disobedience as their Pharisaic teachers. If such respected men could do as they did, why not we? So the

argument went, and so it goes. Do not do as the Pharisees do, Jesus had to say to his disciples, do as they say.

This same Pharisaic leaven is with us today. Even our Anabaptist churches, with their strong emphasis on discipleship, are not free from it. There are scholars and teachers in the church who have made a kind of profession out of writing and speaking about the Anabaptist Vision. They are respected members, not only of a particular denominational party, but of the ecumenical community.

However, it is questionable whether they would have joined the Anabaptists in the sixteenth century, and as of now on their own admission, and for reasons they consider justifiable, do not practice what they advocate. A good friend of mine was critical along similar lines some years ago. In letters which were subsequently published in the fourth issue of *Concern* he wrote: "The bright child of neo-Anabaptism is not adequate—is impotent to make new Anabaptists. . . . Neo-Anabaptism is chiefly academic, an interesting subject to build libraries, journals, lectures around—but not to adopt personally in our daily lives." Ironically, this friend is now in process of building up still another library devoted to the memory of his persecuted forebears. Our Mennonite schools, it seems, do not feel complete without such a collection of Anabaptistica, or at least some sign of loyalty to the Anabaptists of old.

Our Lord himself has taught us to be highly suspicious of this bent toward glorification of the past while rejecting in the present the way pointed to by these heroes of righteousness. Would he not have to say to us, as he walked among our fine libraries, as he witnessed the names of the martyrs of old engraved everywhere over our buildings and institutions, as he saw how we adorn the monuments of the righteous—would he not have to say what he said to the religious leaders of his own time: Woe! Woe to you, scribes and Pharisees, hypocrites!

Several weeks ago, a seminary teacher spoke to me about his deep agony over precisely this point. At a conference where one of the leading exponents of the Anabaptist Vision delivered a challenging address on the need for recapturing in our time the disciplined and disciplining life characteristic of the Anabaptists, he asked at the close of the speech whether the speaker might tell the group something of the way in which the group of Christians with whom he is associated practices these disciplines of which he had just spoken. The question went unanswered, because the speaker did not know from experience such a congregation. The seminary teacher who asked the question is himself deeply convicted that he must find his way to the reality of the Anabaptist Vision or be quiet about it.

Until others are similarly convicted, this kind of hypocrisy will continue to act as a dangerous leaven in our midst, confusing many.

(2) A second hindrance to the kind of straightforward discipleship which, if I understand correctly, is close to the heart of the Christian movement, is one that is difficult to pin down, but is nevertheless a very real menace, especially in our time and in our urbanized culture. I refer to a set of mental and cultural attitudes which we might call "sophistication." Robert Friedmann, who by the way is one of those exponents of the Anabaptist cause who himself has not followed it, but who, to his great merit, frankly admits that he has not, has repeatedly called my attention to this stumbling-block in letters he has written to me during the past few years. He has again and again questioned the possibility of following the disciples' way in the midst of the corroding sophistication of the city. At first, I roundly countered his questioning with familiar theological arguments about the power of the gospel. But now, after seven years of city living, I feel more deeply than ever what he has been trying to say. The mood of our time is an eclectic mood. It is filled with wisdoms and alluring distractions of all kinds. Soon we will have not just eleven TV channels in the Chicago area to select from, but scores of them. We are overwhelmed in our cities with the possibilities of art, music, drama, and dance, experts in this field and that. The communication and travel systems allow us to tune in on all the great and not-so-great minds of our generation.

Not only this, but there is also an almost intangible spirit that begins to possess the atmosphere. One sees it in the attention to style, the shade of the hair, the set of the table, the model and color of the car, the preoccupation with the lawn, and the decorations of the house. What I am talking about requires the sensitivity of a novelist, but all of us must become aware of it. I am calling it here, for want of a better term, sophistication. And I suggest it can eat away at the vital center of what it means to be a Christian, because it takes us away from simple and wholehearted obedience to Jesus. In the midst of all this distraction, not by some great and agonizing rejection, but slowly and imperceptibly Jesus, his words, his example, and his spirit become less important to us.

To be a Christian disciple requires a certain narrowing down. It is not a narrowing that makes us narrow, but like in marriage, a narrowing that is the very fountain of new life. But nevertheless, and definitely, it is a narrowing. If we are serious about going the Christian way, painful sacrifices will have to be made along many unsuspected lines. Our houses may not be as neat, our cars as new, our grades as high, our scholarship as proliferous, our degrees as advanced, our reading as up-to-date, our theater-going as regular, our wardrobe as stylish, our food as fine, and our life as cultured as society around us. And for many this will stand in the way of discipleship as firmly and as definitely as the greatest sin.

I do not need to elaborate on the stories in the gospel where Jesus rebuked just these kinds of things. It will suffice, I am sure, to remind you that not simply bad things frequently kept men back from following Jesus and called forth his urgent warnings but just things like these: enamorment with riches, preoccupation with what to wear and what to eat, attentions to a newly married wife, concern over a new piece of recently purchased property, anxiety about the proper serving of a meal.

I believe this is one of the great temptations of those who are the better-educated members of the church, whose lives will set a certain style, to be emulated by others. What will be the dominating motif of that style? To what will it witness? Will it mark time with the vain sophistries of this age, or shall we cast off all that for the one treasure of wisdom and knowledge which we have in Jesus?

(3) Finally, I want to mention "churchianity" as a barrier to simple obedience to Jesus. If we can imagine again a stranger coming to visit our churches, one who is wholly unfamiliar with the tradition from which they supposedly spring, and who tries now to draw some conclusions about the Christian religion by what he observes, there are certain things that he would, I am sure, quickly conclude. To begin with, he would surely assume that the founder of the Christian movement was a man with strong architectural interests. He might wonder whether the founder did not in fact leave some specific laws in this respect, perhaps a series of commandments, such as: Let my people build themselves buildings for assembly, one building for every two hundred or so. Let them stain the glass and adorn them with crosses. Let them have wooden benches and a raised platform-pulpit in front. And so on. After visiting these buildings and seeing how they are used, our visitor might quickly come to a second conclusion: The founder of the Christian religion had a strong interest in days and seasons and in certain types of assemblies. Here too he might suspect some specific legislation was left behind: Thou shalt meet together for one hour on Sunday morning. Thou shalt hire a speaker, skilled in delivering a discourse not

exceeding a half hour and not less than fifteen minutes. And so forth. And finally, this visitor would surely assume that the founder of this religion was profoundly concerned about the religious instruction of children. Perhaps he commanded: Thou shalt have a Sunday school.

In any case it is undeniable that great numbers of people can barely conceive of the Christian church apart from these three essentials: a religious looking building, a Sunday morning preaching service, and a Sunday school. From my own experience, and from reports of others who have been in on the organization of new congregations, the preoccupation of the religious community with such matters as these is evident even among those considered mature and intelligent members. Lacking a special religious building, lacking a preaching service, lacking a Sunday school, something essential is missing, they feel. Having these, they have what is necessary to a church. It is not that these people do not believe also in other crucial matters, or that their lives do not conform in many respects to the highest ideals of the Christian gospel. It is that they have become attached to something that has little to do with Jesus, something quite harmless in itself. But let it come to occupy such a prominent place in their thinking, and it will tranquilize and protect men from the reality of Jesus himself.

Do we never learn any lessons from history? Do we not see how again and again by their buildings the people of God have been betrayed into false illusions about themselves? Do we not know how the prophets spoke out in the most bitter and passionate way against this fascination with religious buildings and religious services? When I visit even the more modest of these religious sanctuaries, sprouting up everywhere these days, and into which religious people in this country are pouring more than two billion dollars every year, and as I witness the artificiality and superficiality of what frequently goes on there, I hear the words of the prophets of old ringing in my ears: "Who requires of you this trampling of my courts (Isa 1:12).... I hate, I despise your feasts, and I take no delight in your solemn assemblies.... Take away from me the noise of your songs (Amos 5:21, 23)." I am afraid that many of these buildings and much of what goes on in them stands under the judgment of God, are in fact being swept away from the church in many lands, even while we pour out our wealth for them here in America.

But my main point here is that all this becomes a hindrance to a simple and radical obedience to Jesus. So long as we keep these religious buildings and services, so long as we have our Sunday schools, we feel secure. When actually, helpful as these things might be, in themselves they have little to do with Jesus Christ. About the only thing Jesus says concerning religious buildings is to announce judgment on the one so admired by his own disciples and his contemporaries. The only thing he says about worship services is that a day is coming when men will worship, not here in this building or there in that place, but in spirit and in truth. One of the few things he says about children is not that we should educate them but that they should educate us, and for that reason we should hold them close to the bosom and lap of the church. It is not children who need repentance, but we who are adults, Jesus says.

Part II

The gospel that Jesus brings is a many-sided message and looking back on the history of the church one can see that now this side of it, now another side was lost and then in critical hours rediscovered. As I have already intimated, I think one can say that almost always that rediscovery came about in a certain way. There was a man or a woman or a small group of men and women who were gripped by this or that word of Jesus, who felt it penetrate to their inward being, and could not rest until they had obeyed. So Saint Francis listened anxiously for the word of God until hearing the gospel passage where Jesus sends his disciples out on mission with no equipment but the clothes on their back and no message but his message of peace—and off he went. So also William Carey, living in the midst of a church that confined itself for more than a millennium to its European Bastian, felt upon him the command to make disciples of all nations. Had Carey just talked and preached and prophesied among his people at home, it is more than likely not much would have come of it. But at great sacrifice he left the shores of England and acted on what he heard, and through the initial obedience of Carey—and others like him, at first only a small company—the whole Christian church was eventually aroused to its missionary vocation.

Often movements and crises in history at large prepare the people of God for this discovery. For example, the commercial expansion of the trading nations played a part in opening the eyes of the church to its worldwide mission. Carey's obedience spoke so powerfully to his contemporaries because the church was already being spoken to by the Lord of history through this historical development. Similarly, the exhaustion of petty inter-city warfare aroused the concern of many young people in twelfth-century Europe to the crying necessity of peace, and as a consequence the peace-bearing mission of Saint Francis was like a match to explosive dust. From all over Europe young men flocked to his banner. I would like to suggest that in our own time we are on the way to a similar rediscovery of a certain side of Jesus's teaching. And in this too the larger history of our time is playing a decisive part. All parts of world society are undergoing presently an unprecedented social revolution in which the backward and oppressed peoples of the world are demanding a more equal share in the total social welfare. Whether Marxian Communism in the exact form prophesied by Marx and carried out by Lenin wins the world or not, no one can doubt that the Communist Manifesto articulates in many respects the feelings of a vast number of people in our time. From every corner of the globe we hear a cry for justice, a cry of the human family that its members might bear a greater responsibility toward one another, a cry against poverty in the midst of wealth, a cry for a more humane order of society.

It is in this historical struggle that our eyes are being opened, and we are seeing with fresh clarity that side of Jesus's teaching where he speaks of the church as a community of love. It is in this moment that many Christians are rethinking what it means to be part of a people, a people chosen by God in Christ to declare the wonderful deeds of him who called them out of darkness into light (1 Pet 2:9). The Christians of a previous generation were challenged to heroic deeds of service by the missionary summons in Matt 28:18–20, where Jesus bids us go and make disciples of all nations. That mandate is still upon us. But another is forcing its way into our consciousness at this time. It is contained in the words of Jesus in John's Gospel: "By this all men will know that you are my disciples, if you have love for one another" (John 13:35).

Here is the point where I believe the challenge of Jesus is being-felt in a special way. His words are calling into question, at this time especially, the adequacy of our community life as Christians. We are today experiencing an inner disquietude over the lack of reality in our love for one another in the church. And I would like now simply to select several of those words of Jesus in this respect that have spoken to me and I sense to many others over the past several years, and which are challenging us to undertake some unexpected and sometimes rather drastic changes in our manner of life with one another as Christian disciples.

The first of these which I would like to mention is the familiar word of Jesus in Matt 18:20: "For where two or three are gathered together in my name, there am I in the midst of them." I bring this text to your attention first of all because I believe it points us to the very center of that brotherly life we have in Christ, and that is the mystery of Jesus himself present in our midst as a living spirit. One can draw many parallels between a Christian society and other societies, but there will always remain something about a Christian community that will escape the most skilled human sociologist: the presence, the unseen hand, the quickening spirit of the resurrected Lord. For those who have experienced this, this is no theoretical matter. I am sure more times than we realize the resurrected Jesus has helped us in our Fellowship at Reba Place, but there were those times when his help was startlingly apparent even to us, blind as we often are. Israel's deliverance at the Red Sea does not seem strange to those who have had such experiences. Christ walking with his disciples is no longer a far-off event. This is why a Christian community does not make much of human leadership. This is why it lives by that peculiar form of conversation which to an unbelieving observer must look like insanity: prayer. This is why a certain reverence, a quiet awe, a holy expectancy pervades such a community. Jesus the resurrected Lord moves among them, and his nail-pierced hand weaves the pattern of their life together.

But this happens, our text suggests, only among those who have gathered in his name. It is not to any kind of gathering, but to those who unite their lives together in his teaching, his cause, all that his name stands for, that the promise of his presence is given. To know the living Christ in our midst, we must link hands with a specific group of people and allow ourselves to be guided together by the name of Jesus. Here we have what might be called the essentials of a Christian sociology. The Christian movement is a community movement, a group, a fellowship movement. In this respect it is the very opposite of Marxian communism, which aims at the control of mass society through the apparatus of the state and attempts to reorganize society by means of totalitarian power from the top down. It is likewise different from the kind of individualistic, atomistic, *laissez-faire* society some would argue for in the Western world. Unlike both of these, the Christian movement appears in the form of "two or three" gathered together, groups of men and women living with Christ as their guide, with his spirit in their midst. Jesus himself in his earthly ministry chose this way to win the world. Taking a few disciples to himself, he lived with them, taught them, led them. When he had been crucified, raised, and ascended, he breathed into them his spirit. When the number of disciples grew to hundreds and thousands in early Christian times, they continued to form themselves, almost spontaneously it appears, into groups, more at home in a house than in massive sanctuaries. So the church spread, providing wherever it went a deeply personalized home for the men and women it won to the living Lord.

Many secular sociologists are pointing to the disintegration of smaller, more personalized communities in Western society as one source of the delinquency, crime, and emotional instability which are growing so alarmingly. The emergent mass urban cultures with their isolated, uprooted peoples do not answer man's deepest needs, which is to say they do not correspond to the life God intended for man in creation. Realizing this may help us grasp the peculiar necessity and promise of Jesus's words in Matt 18:20 for our time. In these words, Jesus does not invite us to some artificial social contrivance, but rather calls us to live in the way man was meant to live from the beginning: deeply, personally united with a given circle of his fellow men around the center of God's will.

Another familiar text, Matt 18:15, may lead us a step further in understanding the peculiar quality of life that springs up where men and women unite to honor Jesus's name and are guided by his spirit: "If your brother sins, go and tell him his fault between you and him alone. If he listens to you, you have gained your brother." This teaching follows the remarkable parable of the lost sheep and is meant to summarize the significance of that parable for the practical daily life of Christians together. In that parable Jesus points us to the daring love of a shepherd for his sheep, a love that reveals its depths especially at the moment when one of them goes astray. At that moment the shepherd leaves the flock to rescue the lost lamb and experiences a peculiar joy in its restoration. "So," Jesus concludes, "it is not the will of my Father who is in heaven that one of these little ones should perish." Immediately following come the words of this text: "If your brother sins, go."

The text goes on, as you know, to indicate what steps should be taken if the brother refuses to heed the warning brought to him. It culminates in a promise of authority given to the congregation to bind and loose, that is, to determine membership. But I do not want here to go into all the details. I simply want to concentrate on what we can learn from this text about the peculiar love which unites and characterizes a Christian community. We are told here about the kind of sacrificial love that sends a shepherd out after the straying sheep. Or speaking more practically, it is that kind of love that moves one brother to go to another in order to "gain" him back from the bondage of sin. It is a love grounded on the certainty of God's love for every last little one and moved by a deep dedication to the will of God. It is a love that knows the depths of the conflict between good and evil in this world and in the life of the brother. It knows the terrible bondage into which sin can bring a man, and consequently it makes a man willing to sacrifice time and life to save the brother from this bondage.

In John's Gospel we read that Jesus gave his disciples a new commandment. "A new commandment," Jesus said, "I give to you, that you love one another; even as I have loved you, that you also love one another" (John 13:34). I think it can be shown that these important words are only another way of expressing the command in Matt 18:15 that we have been discussing. For how did Christ love his disciples? What is he talking about when he says, "as I have loved you"? In John 15:12, after repeating the new commandment again, Jesus adds, "Greater love has no man than this, that a man lay down his life for his friends." He is referring, of course, to himself. Jesus laid down his life for his friends. But here we must note carefully. In what way did Jesus lay down his life for his disciple-friends? Theologians have sometimes made a great mystery of Jesus's death and avoided that which is most obvious. If we look at the historical facts as they are related to us in the gospels, could it not be said quite simply and truthfully: Jesus was crucified, Jesus laid down his life as a result of practicing the love he teaches us in Matt 18:15. He saw his brothers going astray. He saw them sinning. He came to point out the fault, to win back the lost, and gain them again as brethren. This is the story of the Gospels, how he taught, how he warned and admonished, how he strove to correct and restore the erring ones, and the signs from God that accompanied his ministry. It was in the course of this ministry that he laid down his life. We speak of Jesus as the sin-bearer, and truly he is. But first and foremost in this way. Not in any magical, hocus-pocus way that bypasses the will and personality of man. but as a brother who is so concerned, he came to our side and spoke to us, yes, and kept speaking even when to speak meant retaliation, persecution, and the cross. Even then he did not shrink back from his brotherly responsibility, but practiced what he taught about enemy relations, and absorbed the hostility meted out against him.

What John calls the new commandment, Paul calls the law of Christ. "Bear one another's burdens," he writes to the Galatians, "and so fulfil the law of Christ" (6:2). The reference here is quite explicit. By "the law of Christ" Paul is referring to just that kind of spiritual burden-bearing we have been talking about, where those "who are spiritual," as Paul calls them, seek to restore "a man overtaken" in trespasses and sins. This is the law of Christ, this is the new commandment, this is the root of that practical command in Matt 18:15, "If your brother sins, go." And this is the dynamic spirit of mutual responsibility, the chief mark of that love that unites a Christian community. The Christian community is a fellowship of people who take total liability for one another within their common dedication to God's kingdom and God's righteousness. They are a fellowship of burden-bearers, themselves borne up by the One who bore their sins. They are a community of brothers lifting one another up to the will of God.

This is why it can be said that the greatest offense in the Christian congregation is to let a brother alone in his sin, to pass him by on the other side, perhaps even to gossip about him to another. Contrariwise, the greatest act of love in the Christian congregation is to go and speak to an erring brother about his sin in such a way that he turns away from it and is restored to the will of God. We are never closer to our Master than when we are following him in his ministry of sin-bearing. And he is never so close to us as when we voluntarily get under the burden of a friend floundering in the darkness of sin and seek to bring him back to the light of brotherly love.

It is in this light that we must view the coldness that has settled on many Christian congregations where there has come about an almost complete breakdown of brotherly admonition, warning, and discipline, and men and women meet Sunday after Sunday with their interpersonal hurts unhealed, their sins unconfessed, and in many instances still in bondage to them. Small wonder that our society is sickening at such an alarming pace, churches included.

One of the meaningful experiences of my life during the past seven years has been to discover the profound interrelation between sin, dishonesty, and so-called mental illnesses and to realize the direct relevance of the command of Jesus, under discussion here to this combination of emotionally destructive forces. This discovery took place through a rather literal obedience to Jesus's command to go to a brother when we were concerned or disturbed by something he did. In the course of living by this command we came to see how much hypocrisy had entered into our human relations. Through practicing a strict guard against gossip and speaking out our concerns directly to the person involved, a new openness sprang up among us which allowed for a much freer confession to one another of hidden past sins and mistakes and a facing-up to ourselves as we really know ourselves to be. This exposure helped surprisingly to challenge the evil and strengthen the good within us. A number in our midst who had been in counseling with professional psychologists were significantly helped in this way, and out of this experience we have had a growing ministry to emotionally disturbed people inside and outside of mental hospitals.

In the first letter of John this kind of honest living we are talking about here is called living in the light. I am personally convinced that a great deal of mental illness and emotional instability is the fruit of living in the darkness, of adopting life patterns marked by sin and secrecy, and our churches have for the most part done very little to throw back this darkness because of the timidity of their members in speaking forthrightly and lovingly to one another about sin. We have forgotten that repentance is good news. Jesus, it is said, came preaching the gospel, calling people to repent. The possibility of turning from our deviant, destructive, and socially disastrous ways is good news. It is the gospel entrusted by Jesus to the church, and its relevance was never greater than today in the midst of this emotionally sick and morally confused nation in which we are living. There is no greater task upon us who profess Christianity than to begin practicing this kind of brotherly love where we speak openly to one another of sin and the will of God and seek to help one another along in that inward moral and spiritual transformation without which we will never really live nor be fit to live.

It would be disastrous, however, if our attempt to lay hold of the meaning of life together in Christ would end at this point. So far, we have discussed for the most part the spiritual dimensions of that community life we have in him, that is, its personal and moral dimensions. Our age, however, has grown impatient with the so-called personal and spiritual concerns of the church, and perhaps rightly so, because all too often in its preoccupation with these concerns the church has avoided coming to terms with some of the most obvious needs of men, the need for bread, the need for shelter, the need for medicine and the like. No one can listen to Jesus Christ without becoming aware of the priority of the moral and personal over the material. At the same time no one can read the New Testament without realizing that the common life in Christ has a profound effect upon the material side of life.

It is with this in mind that I would like to call your attention to a final passage for our consideration, some words of Jesus which I first encountered about ten years ago and which helped me grasp at that time his concern for the bearing of love on the material side of life. They are the words we find in

Luke 12:32, "Fear not, little flock, for it is your Father's good pleasure to give you the kingdom. Sell your possessions and give alms; provide yourselves with purses that do not grow old, with a treasure in the heavens that does not fail, where no thief approaches and no moth destroys. For where your treasure is, there will your heart be also."

A year or so after discovering these words I wrote an article based on them. I entitled the article, "A Hard Saying." Some have said that words like these are not simply hard, but impossible. They suggest that at this point Jesus was carried away by his own eschatological excitement, and proposed conduct that could not but lead to economic disaster over any but the briefest period of time. My own thinking about these words has changed somewhat in the years since I wrote that first article, but not in the direction indicated by the word "impossible," rather in the direction suggested by the word "gospel." For here too experience teaches that Jesus is speaking to us not so much about something hard, although so it may seem as we take the first steps in carrying it out, but about grace, about our deliverance from a false way of thinking and living.

If we examine the various places where Jesus speaks about economic matters, a rather simple, clear message emerges, one which surely we should understand today, if ever, and one which has immediate relevance for our present age. We can summarize this message, I believe, under three points.

Point one: God wants to give us the kingdom; "Fear not little flock, for it is your Father's good pleasure to give you the kingdom." The point here is that God will take care of our material needs as we seek first his kingdom and his righteousness. It is a point many skeptics have derided. Even many Christians have questioned it. And yet it is an assertion that Jesus makes so often and so passionately that we must consider it one of the most vital parts of the message he brings to us. Look at the lilies, he says how God clothes them. Are you not worth far more than lilies? Look at the birds. Not a sparrow falls outside the watchful knowledge of God. Are you not worth more than sparrows? The hairs of your head are numbered. In these and other ways Jesus makes the point that God watches over and cares for the material side of life and delights in caring for us as we seek his will.

Point two of Jesus's teaching on the material side of life is the fruit of this faith in the fatherly care of God: trustful renunciation. In place of the fear, anxiety, and fretting that marks the heathen world's attitude toward property, Jesus calls us to renounce, to sell out, to say goodbye to our property. This renunciation is not done as a purely negative thing, but as the first act of trust. It is the fruit of our first awakening to the message of God's love and the condition of following on into the life of discipleship. "Whoever of you does not renounce all that he has," Jesus said one time to a crowd that followed him, "cannot be my disciple" (Luke 14:33).

The word renunciation is not much used in Christian circles today. We have substituted a word that Jesus never used in this connection, the word stewardship. This has allowed us to perpetuate an attitude toward property that makes the final point of Jesus's teaching with regard to property seem absurd. The word stewardship tends to encourage a man to feel an even greater attachment to his property than he otherwise might, by giving him a sense of religious responsibility for it. It tends to exalt the wealthy who supposedly have been given their wealth as a trust from God. But Jesus did not speak of our stewardship of wealth but of renouncing it, of breaking free from its service and standing ready to sell it and distribute it to the poor.

That is the third point in Jesus's teaching: distribution—the point where the scandal of what he says in the other points becomes visible. Every great prophet from the days of Moses, through Amos, Hosea, Isaiah, Jeremiah, on down to John the Baptist spoke out for economic justice, for distribution and sharing. So far as I can understand the words of Jesus, he is only making the same point. He is laying the spiritual groundwork for a community where distribution and sharing of wealth will come as naturally as breathing. He came announcing the year of Jubilee, the glad day of distribution when all members of the community again were to have equal access to the material necessities of life. This is what Jesus means when he speaks of laying up treasures in heaven, of providing ourselves with purses that do not grow old. To the rich young ruler, he says: "Sell all that you have and distribute to the poor, and you will have treasure in heaven, and come follow me" (Luke 18:22). The way to lay up treasures in heaven is to distribute to the poor on earth.

This is what we see the early Christians doing according to Luke's well-known account in the Acts of the Apostles. I know of no better commentary on the teachings of Jesus touching on material affairs than the description there: "And no one said that any of the things which he possessed was his own, but they had everything in common" (Acts 4:32). "And all who believed were together and had all things in common; and they sold their possessions and goods and distributed them to all, as any had need" (Acts 2:44–45).

Here we can glimpse as clearly as anywhere the meaning of the love Christians have for one another, as it affects the material side of life. That we see so few examples in our time of this kind of voluntary economic sharing of rich and poor among Christian people is another one of the signs of the loss of love among us, and, as many now recognize, one of the reasons for the rapid spread of secular and violent communism across the earth. The hour is late, but certainly not too late to recover this side of things again among Christian people. Who knows what leavening effect it will have, if we do this, upon the history of our time. Men may seem callous, yet they also seem hungry for the reality of a truly just and humane existence.

There would be much more to say about this and other matters we have touched on, but I would like to close by returning to a theme which I have mentioned repeatedly: our obedience. Has Jesus Christ, the One we profess to serve, been saying anything to us? Has some new truth, some new issue of discipleship been growing upon us? Have we felt him disturbing us, perhaps laying his finger upon some sin or disobedience in our own lives, or showing us where in our participation in the Christian church we have been lacking? Everything depends on whether we heed that call. The on-going, not to speak of the renewal of the Christian moment, is at stake. We can multiply discussions like this, and fill the world with lectures and books, but the future of the church of Jesus Christ will be determined by none of these without concrete acts of obedience in conformity to the word and spirit of the Master.

11

Marginalia: A Syllabus of Issues

JOHN HOWARD YODER

Since its No. 5 in 1958, *Concern* has carried the subtitle "Pamphlet Series on Questions of Christian Renewal." Yet this number is the first to carry papers written specifically on the theme of renewal. Neither was written first of all for *Concern*; in original audience, purpose, and character they are quite varied. This made it difficult to carry on a further exchange between the two authors, because of differences in conversational style more than in substance. We have therefore had to build the bridge in the form of a "study guide" to the two papers. In view of their difference in character, this study cannot be a simple comparative balancing of equivalent theses: it must seek to discern the decisive issues behind the diversity of styles.

Leland Harder's Basic Stance

The Harder paper was prepared for a discussion within the faculties of the Associated Mennonite Biblical Seminaries, in the framework of a series of studies in the foundations of curriculum. Topics were phrased very broadly and included reporting on "what is going on" in current publications within the teacher's field of responsibility. It is thus understandable that Harder does not preface his reporting with a clear evaluative commitment. We must read carefully to see him taking sides at all through much of the first section. The first and third "indictments" (establishment and residential limits) are left with no judgment as to their weight; the second (success-seeking) is blunted by a shifting "trend in debate."

In the second section the stance shifts somewhat. The "rugged individualist" position reported for Berger is rejected in the name of the Anabaptist doctrine of the church. The mediant "renewal" position, "expanding the work of the church in the world" with "de-emphasis of concentration on intra-church program" is challenged for another kind of reason: because its proponents are unable to explain why the changes they advocate are sufficient to regain the authenticity of the church. But then the third prescription—reformation—is rejected as well in a three-sentence turn of the argument. One sentence says that the difference between symptoms and causes is only a matter of time; the second appeals to "biblical perspective" and the third locates the sin of presumption among the critics of existing churches who deny the evidence that God is at work. (The paper does not make clear where these evidences have been recorded or why advocates of re-formation must deny them.)

One fruitful line of meditation for the reader may well be to recirculate in his mind the variety of criteria here at work, and to ask whether the successive rejection of all three prescriptions adds up, as suggested by the Wagoner quote, to an inference that all the indictments are wrong after all.

A second phase of this meditation would then move on to Harder's third and briefest section, the ten-point list of marks of authenticity. How do these Anabaptist-oriented standards compare and contrast with the three indictments and the three prescriptions? Would their consistent application support Harder's rejection of all three "prescriptions"? Would they support, reject, or refocus the indictments? Do they support the leanings Harder expresses regarding the five "ambiguities" in the fourth section?

Leland Harder's New Forms

The sample proposal for a congregation in a psychiatric center, being the only concrete one in the paper, may reward closer analysis. Though introduced with references to Colin Williams' advocacy of "taking the shape of the world's needs," it differs significantly from Williams.

a. Williams envisages varied congregational forms side by side, keeping the residential churches for prayer, preaching, and sacraments, using the "forms of need" only as a frame for mission. But Harder would go further and transfer the "instituted means of grace" right into the hospital congregation. Judging by the preceding list of "marks," this will include some kind of defined membership and discipline.

One can make a case for this centering of all churchly functions in one structure, rather than letting several types of centers run competitively in parallel. But to argue this is to reject the distinction between "instituted" and "prudential" means of grace, which Harder accepts elsewhere. In forsaking Williams' pattern in favor of the psychiatric center with membership and sacraments, Harder raises (especially after recognizing the Anabaptist concept of membership) a host of new problems. Would the spouses (and children?) of staff and patients also belong to the congregation, or would they be gathered elsewhere around some other need? What would be the functional equivalent of baptism or the church letter? How would the treatment of member and non-member patients differ? How will the corporate discipline relate to the therapist's respect for the varieties of his patients' moral attitudes?

b. Nothing in Williams' list of possible groupings[1] indicates that the form of such a "world-shaped" fellowship should be that of a specialized service institution with its administrative hierarchy, financial structure, real estate, and prescribed professional services. His vision of a small group of people doing unusual, undone, voluntary, exploratory jobs together is close to the center of his concept of mission. But even if Williams' thought could be stretched at this point, one must doubt whether the ten marks of authenticity could. How should making no formal distinctions between categories of membership and leadership relate to the hospital's distinction between doctors and patients, or even between doctors and nurses? How will "meeting of all human need through the sharing of money" correlate with the center's fee and salary structures?

c. Harder proposes that the matrix of the congregation should be a church-related institution. This may facilitate the experiment, but would it not also reduce proportionately its exemplary value? Most of the world's needs do not have that shape. Williams would think rather of Christians working within non-church agencies. Does Harder mean, or does he not, that we could expect the authorities in a state mental hospital to permit the formation of a believers' church in their "house," encompassing some staff and some patients, baptizing, witnessing, covenanting, and disciplining with religious authority?

1. Williams, *Where in the World*, 59.

d. But with all this movement away from Williams, Harder does not challenge his assumptions at the point where the Anabaptist-Free Church position might. Williams' concept of the "residential parish" is the one left over from the age of Christendom; a sociological unit, defined geographically, which the church services with a sort of chaplaincy function, inserting moral values and spiritual resources as she can, with or without the committed collaboration of all its parishioners. In modern society, where geography is no longer the most important social subdivision, other lines will dictate other "parishes"—the school, the factory, the supermarket, the resort—but the parish church's function is still the old one. She teaches moral values, tries to steer social change in a wholesome direction, motivates, and celebrates. Whether individual lives are transformed from aimlessness or selfishness to obedience is not the major issue, although it would be welcomed. Even without "making converts" the missionary imperative may be faithfully fulfilled within the ministry of those already committed to activities in the parish.

Perhaps because he took rural Mennonitism as a valid sample, Harder did not point out that for the Free Church the parish pattern never was normative. The Free Church does not consider any one social group its "parish"; even before modern transportation, congregations were made up of many who traveled a good distance. Free Church members always found "getting together" a problem; newer travel possibilities make this easier, not harder. (So does modern residential mobility; if moving is guided by the church's concerns, as every major direction of life should be, the urban principle of "communal isolation" is not an inexorable law. Those who choose to be able to meet can do so more easily than in other ages). Even those Mennonite urban church-building efforts which (properly) make special effort to be accessible to their immediate neighbors find themselves developing congregations in which many of the members drive from elsewhere. But the residential parish was disregarded by the Free Church long before the "neighborhood" was relativized by urbanization.

Thus, an Anabaptist-oriented renewal concern might be cautious about the parish approach to the structures of contemporary society, not because it is too radical, but because it is still the "chaplaincy to Christendom" and not the communion of the saints. Anabaptist congregationalism would have no objection to Christian task forces to sharpen their faithfulness in serving and witnessing within the hospital, the factory, the university; but it would want the primary fellowship center of these Christians to include brethren and sisters of other gifts, loyalties, and perspectives, with whom all dimensions of life would be shared.

John Miller's Indictment: Apostasy

According to the critics whom Harder quotes, the churches of our day are boring, sanctimonious, dishonest, irrelevant, sluggish, fit to serve only the aged and sick and emotionally crippled. Yet they can still be called churches.

Miller's paper was presented to the second Student Services Summer Seminar for graduate students, at Elkhart in August 1964, in the framework of a concentrated study of Anabaptist origins and contemporary concerns. The assignment, contrary to that of the Harder paper, was to be radically pointed. Miller begins immediately by introducing other categories. He would substitute the biblical terms "apostasy" and "judgment"' for the sociologists' labels. Not all who say "Lord, Lord" are known by the Lord: not all "churches" are church. The alternative is not to be "insipid" or "irrelevant" but to be condemned.

What would it mean to insert the concepts of apostasy and judgment into the frame of Harder's analysis? Would this simply compound the presumptuousness of which he accuses the friends of reformation? Would Harder argue biblically against the use of these categories? What would a strong concept of apostasy like Miller's say to Harder 's choosing to quote critics only from the ranks of mainstream ecumenical, academically respectable Protestantism?

John Miller's Diagnosis: Hypocrisy

A further common trait of all Harder's sources is that they discuss sociological structures and their modification without reference to the presence or absence of personal devotion and obedience on the part of given individuals. Do the sociologists assume, or do they not, that proper structures will work, quasi-automatically, and improper ones will not?

Harder comes closest to the issue of obedience-hypocrisy in the discussion of the last two "ambiguities"—essence and form. But both times the treatment shifts to a comparison not between essence and forms but between forms and other forms (prudential and instituted, the various meanings of "local").

Is it possible in principle, or is it not, for sociology to deal with the quality of personal obedience as a variable? Peter Berger is once cited as interested in "making Christ normative for ethics." This might be a hint that Miller's desiderata—obedience, a different style of life (cars and houses not so neat, life not so cultured, scholarship not so advanced, etc.), a peculiar kind of love especially for the deviant, and a full reorientation of economic reflexes—would be sociologically measurable. Then hypocrisy, i.e., the capacity for self-deception in order to avoid the crisis of repentance, is also a sociological fact.

What then would it mean to introduce this dimension into Harder's survey? Might the various "prescriptions" be further evaluated by the measure of their facilitating the discovery and the healing of hypocrisy?

Thus Saith the Lord

Obedience presupposes a clear knowability of the will of God. Miller sees this will clearly expressed in the words of Jesus in the Gospels. Many theologies would hold this to be an oversimplification:

- because the Gospels, they say, and especially Matthew's, distort the teachings of the historic Jesus through legalistic concerns;

- because the Logos-Christ of John's Gospel or the cosmic Christ of Paul call for a more affirmative attitude to the structures and cultural values of this world;

- or because the patient, gracious Christ of Protestant theology would not be so hard on people, especially not on persons of limited capacities, as to ask of them an unrealistically high level of moral achievement.

This is the most clearly theological issue we can leave to the careful reader. Are the several "Christs" as different as such a critique supposes? If they are, on what grounds would one choose among them? Is Miller 's focusing on the synoptic Jesus a legitimate simplification, in view of the intended concise challenge to a specific audience? Or are the other Christs so different as to make this fore-shortening illegitimate? Which Christ is presupposed by Harder's various options?

Opposite Miller 's radical "Thus saith the Lord," Harder represents objectivity and experimental tentativeness. Are his proposals made more or less likely to succeed by their experimental label? Or by coordination, recruitment, and subsidy on the conference level?

The Christian Style of Life

Harder and Miller agree, in radical difference from most Christian traditions, in making obedience a test of the church's authenticity. Harder bases this on the assumption, which his paper was not asked to justify, of an Anabaptist perspective; Miller bases it on the words of Jesus. Is this a significant difference, or only a formal one? If the two authors were asked to debate, there would obviously be further differences as to the substance of ethics, as for instance between "stewardship" and "renunciation" as economic attitudes. But, without asking them, does the reader discern any fundamental difference between the Harder marks of authenticity and Miller's selection of some words of Jesus that have contemporary relevance?

Concern's purpose to serve as a forum has hitherto not been expressed so directly in a juxtaposition of views on the same theme. Further serious contributions would be gratefully received.

12

The Order that Belongs to the Gospel

Lewis Benson

The religion of the Bible is not only concerned with the relation of the individual to God but with the relation of God to God's people. For each individual, God has designed an ordered, holy life that is based on hearing and obeying his word. But God has also designed an ordered community life for the people who live by his word.

Both the Old and the New Testaments deal with the order that belongs to God's people. The central feature of the ordered life of God's people in the Old Testament was God's holy law. In time this law became objectified into a complicated legal code with an immense literature of interpretation and a permanent staff of lawyers.

The spiritual vitality of this people depended largely on the presence of called and qualified spokesmen for God—the prophets. When no prophets appeared for generations, or even centuries, the life of the people became dominated by a class of priestly administrators with vested interests who often became the traditional opposers of the prophets. Thus, the prophetic element was continually being weakened by the spirit of legalism and the spirit of institutionalism. The later prophets began to look toward a future time when God's people would live by God's law without human mediation and when God's kingly rule would be truly established among them.

The coming of Christ was interpreted by the first Christians as the fulfillment of these expectations. Jesus began his ministry with the words: "The time is fulfilled, and the kingdom of God is at hand: repent ye, and believe the gospel." And Paul says, "We declare unto you glad tidings, how that the promise which was made unto the fathers, God hath fulfilled the same unto us their children, in that he hath raised up Jesus again."[1]

The "good tidings" are not only concerned with reconciliation of the individual soul to God, but they have to do also with a new covenant between God and his people which brings a new kind of order to God's people. George Fox says, "Christ bid His disciples 'Go preach the gospel unto all nations': and since this was done are many gathered into the fellowship and order of it."[2] The new covenant does not become known through a new law. Jesus did not come primarily to reconstitute the Hebrew code of morals but to proclaim the good news. The order of the new covenant is not to be found in a series of ordinances which Jesus, as the "Founder" of Christianity, instituted during his lifetime. The new order is not the consequence of Jesus's teaching but the consequence of his death and resurrection. The first church was gathered through the preaching of the resurrection, and it was community—gathered around and to the resurrected Lord. In the old covenant, God gave his people ten laws, but in the new covenant, God gives not a new law but a divine Lawgiver. God's voice commands from heaven, "This is my beloved Son . . . hear him."

The new order is based on the presence of the living Christ in the midst of his people exercising his offices as their living Prophet and Priest and King. The church is based on Christ's promise, "I will not leave you comfortless: I will come to you." There is no church except where Christ is present. It is Christ's presence that brings order. He is the Orderer of his people in two ways: first, through his offices as Prophet, Priest, and King, but also as Bishop, Counselor, Teacher, Leader, and Guide of his people; and second, through the spiritual gifts that he gives to every member. In exercising his offices and giving gifts to every member, Christ gives an orderly corporate life to his people that is not dependent on the existence of organizational machinery of any kind.

The question "Did Jesus found a church?" is based on a misunderstanding. The church is not a projection into history of something that Jesus established in his lifetime. This would relegate Christ's work as the Orderer of his church to what he did in the first century. It is not only because of what Christ once did but also because of what he now does that the new order for God's people becomes a possibility. Christ is related to

---

1. Mark 1:15; Acts 13:32–33.
2. Fox, *Works*, 8:129.

his church not as its Hero-Founder but in a fresh and living way that is perennially new.

The rejection of the idea that Jesus intentionally founded an ecclesiastical institution and defined its internal order by a series of ordinances does not mean that Jesus was unconcerned about a continuing community. Jesus said, "The law and the prophets were until John: since that time the kingdom of God is preached and every man presseth into it."[3] And again he said, "I appoint unto you a kingdom, as my Father hath appointed unto me."[4] Jesus predicted that the band of itinerant disciples would scatter, but he also described the coming community of the new Israel. It was to be a community that was in the world but by the power of God was kept from the evil that is in the world. It had a unity that is God-given. It was persecuted for righteousness' sake. It was like a community of lambs among wolves. It was hated as Jesus was hated. It experienced in its corporate life the redemptive power of suffering for Christ's sake.

Jesus used the term "gospel" in announcing his mission and ministry. In Luke, Jesus quoted Isaiah: "The Spirit of the Lord is upon me, because he has anointed me to preach good news to the poor. He has sent me to proclaim release to the captives and recovering of sight to the blind, to set at liberty those who are oppressed, to proclaim the acceptable year of the Lord."[5] The Lord's acceptable year was proclaimed and the time declared to be at hand when Israel's hope of the coming kingdom would be fulfilled. The expected new covenant and new kingdom and new prophet and new priest and new king were at hand. This was the good news.

The power of the tempter, the deceiver, the evil one was to be broken; and mankind, whom he had captivated and blinded, was to be set free and given sight. This was the good news. In the new order which was about to break forth there was to be a new liberty such as was nowhere experienced or even possible under the old covenant. The order that belonged to the gospel was not only deliverance from the power of the evil one, but it was deliverance from the imperfections and weakness of the old covenant.

"Behold, all things are become new" meant a new order for God's people. This newness was not the newness of a revolution but of fulfillment. It was not that the old covenant was evil but that it was unfinished or incomplete. It was a preparatory stage for that which was to come later and

---

3. Luke 16:16.
4. Luke 22:29.
5. Luke 4:18–19.

"fulfill" it. Christ's church was not an anarchy. It had an order within it. But what was the nature of this order? Since Reformation times four answers have been given to this question.

The first type of answer comes from churches that follow the teaching of Luther. Here the church is seen as a human institution. From this viewpoint the "true church" is invisible and the visible church always bears the marks of its human authorship. But this visible church must guard against corrupting influences and by a process of continual self-examination and revision, it must keep itself as free from corruptions as is humanly possible.

The second type of answer comes from the "free spirits" of the sixteenth century. These regard the invisible church as alone representing the church of the New Testament, and they regard visibility as a sign of apostasy. They are individualists who make no contribution to the question of church order.

The third approach springs from the extreme Bible-centeredness of the Reformation and finds expression in the Anabaptists who challenged the Reformers to carry the reformation of the church to its logical conclusion along Biblical lines. This view assumes that God intends his church to be a visibly gathered community of believers and that such a community existed in apostolic times. It sees the historical church as fallen and apostatized and seeks its "restitution" in terms of a restoration of the pattern of church life described in the New Testament.

The fourth approach also assumes that God intends his church to be a visibly gathered community of believers. And yet the approach of this group—the Quakers—is based on a different principle of Christian renewal from that of the Anabaptists. The Quakers do not understand the "fall of the church" in terms of departure from the pattern of church life as described in the New Testament. The apostasy, they say, was not from originally established forms and norms, but from the perennial and ever fresh possibility in the gospel dispensation for God's people to become ordered by a living Orderer and Governor who is in their midst. From the Quaker viewpoint the most careful imitation of first-century church life is also a kind of apostasy because it is not the right way to find God's order for God's people under the gospel. The gospel not only brings a new order, but it also brings a new way of finding and maintaining that order.

When Fox says that the foundation of our Quaker meetings is Christ,[6] he does not mean that Quaker church order is founded on certain

---

6. Fox, *Works*, 8:79.

ordinances or teachings of the historical Christ. He means that it is founded on an experience of the risen Christ as he is actually present in the midst of his church as its divine Orderer. For Fox, apostasy is a rejection of Christ in all his offices: "There is no true church, " he says, "but where Christ is exercising all His offices. . . . Now the everlasting gospel is preached again, and many are gathered into the gospel by the power of God and are turned to the light which is the life in Christ, are grafted into Him, and are come to walk in the order of the New Covenant."[7]

Quakerism is not a new attempt to apply the principles of that Reformation that was begun in the sixteenth century, and it does not share some of the basic presuppositions of that Reformation. It can only be rightly understood in terms of a new departure in the story of Christian renewal.

This new departure is based on a fresh interpretation of the "gospel" in terms of the witness of the whole Bible. In the Bible man's predicament does not consist in his failure to realize his full potential. It involves sin, which is an act of rebellion against the God of truth and a following of the world's God in whom there is no truth. But though God is sinned against he is steadfast in his love and answers man's rebellion with promises of redemption. He promises that the deceiver will be overthrown, and he promises the regathering of the community of the blessed which will fill the whole earth.

The establishment of God's righteousness and God's rule in human affairs is the great vision and hope of those whom God calls to be the children of the promises. The hope of Israel becomes embodied in the phrase, "the kingdom of God."

Jesus's proclamation, "The time is fulfilled," means that the time had come for the fulfillment of God's promises and of Israel's hope. The "good news" means that that which had been lost is now to be restored, namely, the righteousness which God teaches and the community over which he rules. A new righteousness has come which is not the righteousness of a written code but the righteousness which is learned at the feet of a living Teacher. A new community has come which is not a religious institution, but which has an ordered, articulate life centered on the living Christ. The living Christ is the chief cornerstone of the new covenant community. This is the stone which has been rejected by all the wise master builders of man-made religion.

The new Israel is not a religious institution established by a founder and maintained by a succession of orthodox administrators. It is not a

---

7. Fox, *Journals*, 2:36.

cultus with a worship ritual and with initiation, marriage, and burial ceremonies. It has no priestly hierarchy or clerical class that stand opposed to the laity. It has no creedal basis for membership and no sacred Scriptures that must be accepted as supreme authority.

The order of this community is God-given, not manmade. It does not stand in relation to the religious communities of the world as a species is related to a genus. It is the unique order that belongs to the new covenant and to the gospel.

Therefore, from the Quaker viewpoint, the task of Christian renewal does not consist in the restoration of the church of the apostolic age, but it consists in becoming directly related to Christ in a master-disciple relationship and finding through this relationship fellowship with one another as God's people in the new covenant.

The Christ of whom the Bible bears witness is a living Being whose fellowship-forming power can be known by all who answer his call to discipleship. The supreme reality for the Christian man is to obey Christ, and the mark of the community of those who obey Christ is their readiness to suffer and to accept the reproaches of the unregenerate world.

The inner life of this community is ordered by means of the gifts that Christ gives to all the members of his church. Each one has his gift and his service. All are priests—both men and women.

The good news is not that the Christian religion has come but that Christ has come. The order that belongs to this good news is not a new constitution and bylaws, but it centers around One who gives himself eternally to be the Head of God's people and to impart righteousness without legalism and community without institutionalism. In this community there is order, equality, unity, liberty, righteousness, joy, and peace in the spirit and the corporate experience of the redemptive power of suffering.

What are some of these qualities of the new covenant community? George Fox says, "All true liberty is in the gospel." What is this gospel liberty? At the beginning of his ministry Jesus announces that he has come to fulfill the prophecy that promised deliverance to the captives and to set at liberty those that are broken and shattered.[8] He declares that it is truth that brings freedom, but he defines truth as that which is imparted to those who "continue in my word" and "are truly my disciples."[9]

---

8. Luke 4:18–19.
9. John 8:31–32.

In the New Testament "truth" is not the opposite of error, but the opposite of sin. Sin is not merely "falling short," "missing the mark," or "mistakenness." It is belief in a lie and the words of a liar. Insofar as human life has become dominated by a lie, the captive state has come to be the condition of mankind.

The lie appears in its most insidious form when it reaches us in the guise of religion. In institutional religion the liar can offer comfort, security, and a kind of order in place of the voice of God's heavenly prophet, Jesus Christ. The liar has his captives inside organized religion as well as outside it.

Christ restores to man the experience of hearing and obeying the pure wisdom from above and liberates from captivity those who have believed the lie. Fox says, "Christ the truth destroyeth the destroyer, the devil, and bruises the head of him that hath people in bondage . . . and so it is Christ the truth that doth set free."[10] "Christ saith, 'If the Son makes you free, you will be free indeed,' free from the devil . . . free from all false ways, false worship, and teachers, free from being subject to the serpent . . . [and] so free men and free women to serve the Lord in the new life. . . . So serve the Lord as free men and women and there is your joy, peace, [and] comfort and that which makes you free is the truth, and the truth is Christ who destroys the devil and his works."[11]

This freedom is not individualism; it is freedom in a unique community. Fox says, "they that obey the voice of the Lord . . . and Christ Jesus . . . come into unity and fellowship with one another . . . and in this they know the order of Christ and [know] God to be a God of order."[12] The liberty with which Christ makes us free is liberty in community. In this ordered community in which there is true liberty there is also power. The power of the gospel order is power to overcome the power of the deceiver. "Behold," says Jesus, "I give . . . you power . . . over all the power of the enemy."[13] And Paul says that the gospel and the kingdom come not in word only but in power.[14]

Fox says: "the fellowship is in the power—not in the form."[15] He proclaims, "Now is the redeeming and recovering of things that were in the apostles' days and now the gospel of God is known and the power of God

10. Fox, "George Fox's Epistles," 315(8, 90F).
11. Fox, Henry J. Cadbury Papers, 29(58E).
12. Fox, *Works*, 8:184.
13. Luke 10:19.
14. 1 Cor 4:20; 1 Thess 1:5.
15. Fox, *Works*, 5:105.

. . . and now . . . is the fellowship known by which shall all the . . . fellowships upon earth be broken which are not in the power."[16]

"[They] may say (who have told the world they are orthodox men) 'What, have we not had the gospel all this while?' I say, 'No . . . [because] they went from the power of God which is the gospel.'"[17] This power is the power to stand firm in the truth that Christ teaches and to suffer the consequences of nonconformity to the world. It is not merely some extraordinary psychic phenomenon, but the power to withstand sin. This power is not only given to the disciples of Christ individually, but also to the community that is gathered in his name. They are brought into unity and strength and corporate moral solidarity by a power that comes from Christ. When persecution comes, they do not scatter but stand and suffer for the sake of Christ and his kingdom.

Jesus teaches that discipleship and the cross belong together. Fox says: "to the cross, the power of God, all must bend and bow,"[18] and all the poorness and emptiness and barrenness is in the state that man is in in the fall, out of the power of God; by which power he is made rich and hath strength again, which power is the cross."[19]

"The Lord is coming to bring His people . . . to know that the power of God is the cross of Christ which crucifies them to the world."[20]

"Living by the power of the cross leads men to Christ. . . . The power being lived in the cross is lived in, and whenever Friends come into this . . . they leave a witness behind them answering the witness of God in others."[21]

The fellowship of disciples is a fellowship in the cross. The church that does not know the cross is apostate. Fox said, "There hath been an apostasy in the whole of Christendom from the cross of Christ which is the power of God."[22] "In the apostasy," he says, "the gospel was lost among them and the government of Christ,"[23] and he exhorts the Quakers to "know the cross of Christ which is the power of God, which crucifies from the state in the

---

16. Fox, *Works*, 4:229.
17. Fox, *Works*, 4:228.
18. Fox, *Works*, 7:218.
19. Fox, *Journal*, 1:346.
20. Fox, *Works*, 2:297.
21. Fox, *Journal*, 2:328–30.
22. Fox, *Annual Catalogue*, 64.
23. Fox, *Works*, 8:59, 60.

apostasy."[24] "[For] . . . you are gathered out of the apostasy and over it into the everlasting gospel order as was in the apostles' days . . . which gospel order was not of man nor by man but by Christ the spiritual man."[25]

For the disciple church, fellowship and unity are experienced through the cross. "The cross, the power of God," says Fox, "keeps all in order, subjection, and humility."[26] In this church "all . . . walk in unity over the enmity."[27] In time of persecution or trouble the bonds of this church of the cross are strengthened. They are like the walls built to resist earthquakes that become stronger and more compacted with every shock. "Let us thank God," said the author of Hebrews, "that we have received a kingdom that cannot be shaken."

The unity that comes through the cross is experienced through obedience and through suffering. Of this corporate obedience Fox says, "They that do obey the voice of the Lord . . . and Christ Jesus . . . come into unity and fellowship one with another and with the Son and with the Father; and in this they know the order of Christ, and God to be a God of order."[28]

"In this day of the power of Christ all His people are made a willing people."[29]

"This is the perfect love and perfect oneness in the perfect unity with the Father and the Son and with His church; and this oneness is that which convinces the world, that the world may know that God hath sent His Son, by the love and unity and oneness that is amongst the saints."[30]

The unity of the cross is experienced in the suffering that comes to the church as a consequence of obedience to Christ. Bonhoeffer says, "As it follows Christ, suffering becomes the church's lot too." This unity in suffering and in obedience to the righteousness taught by Christ leads to nonconformity to the world. "Where the world is left standing, the cross is not lived in," says Fox.[31] The Lord is coming, he says, "to bring His people . . . to know that the power of God is the cross of Christ which crucifies them to

---

24. Fox, *Works*, 7:264.
25. Fox, *Works*, 8:84.
26. Fox, *Journal*, 2:340.
27. Fox, *Works*, 7:322–23.
28. Fox, *Works*, 8:184.
29. Fox, *Journal*, 2:432.
30. Fox, *Works*, 5:292.
31. Fox, *Works*, 7:66.

the world,"[32] and he reminds the faithful that "they that followed Christ in His cross, they were strangers to the world."[33]

In this fellowship of the cross there is discipline and order. To the institutionalists it looks like utter chaos and anarchy. Nobody is "heading things up," there are no written rules binding on all members and there appears to be no objective authority. Fox likens the spirit of institutionalism to the spirit that caused Nimrod to build Babel—a city to preserve him and his people after the flood. "But God did confound them and their work and so He will do [to] all such builders. For you see how God did confound all the Jewish builders, yea, the wise master builders who rejected Christ the cornerstone and His order, and His government and council."[34] Christ is the Author of the church's order and discipline, he is its Orderer and it is responsible to him. All authority resides in him. The rule of Christ is not only experienced on the level of the local congregation. Christ is the head of the whole church. Wherever any gather together in his name to wait upon him, there is the church and there it is possible to know the order of the gospel. This is true whether the gathering is local, regional, national, or international.

What the priests and prophets and kings were to God's people in the old covenant, Christ is to God's people in the new covenant. Looking to Christ and following him in obedience of faith is the new and living way. Christ "makes all things new and redeems out of the earth," says Fox. "Here Christ walks in the midst of His church which sings the new song . . . which none can learn but they who are redeemed by Christ out of the earth."[35]

Christ gives gifts to every member of his church and each member in the exercise of his gift makes an offering that contributes to the harmonious working of the whole body. "The least member of the church hath an office and is serviceable; and every member hath need one of another,"[36] said Fox. But it is Christ who calls and qualifies his elders, overseers, ministers, teachers, prophets, record keepers, evangelists, missioners, etc. His order can be seen in the harmonious working together of those whom he has called. He chooses his own workmen for each particular task. He supplies the needs of the church through the gifts that he gives to his members.

32. Fox, *Journal*, 2:297.
33. Fox, *Works*, 7:16.
34. Fox, *Works*, 8:137.
35. Fox, Henry J. Cadbury Papers, 179 (15, 39G).
36. Fox, *Works*, 7:347.

So here is an order. It is the order for which man was created. It results from hearing and obeying the voice of the Creator. This order is possible for us only through the gospel.

In this ordered community there is liberty, righteousness, unity, peace, joy, the redemptive power of suffering for the sake of Christ and his kingdom, and nonconformity to the world. It is to this community that the testimony of the prophets and apostles directs us. Christ himself is the chief cornerstone.

The Quaker approaches the problem of Christian renewal in a frame of reference that is different from that of the Reformers of the sixteenth century. The Quaker does not take as his chief presupposition the Reformers' principle of the supreme authority of the Bible, his approach is based on a new principle. It is a direct appropriation of the gospel truth that Christ has come, that he is now alive and ready to appear in the midst of any community of disciples to give his order, which is the order that belongs to the gospel, to those who look to him alone as their Head and Supreme Authority, and Orderer.

This approach to Christian renewal accounts for most of those things by which the Quaker fellowship has been distinguished from other types of church fellowships. This includes such things as authority in church government, ministry, pastoral care, and worship; nonconformity to the world in dress, speech, and giving honor to men; testimonies against war, luxurious living, and judicial oaths; and Christian practices relating to marriages and burials. The sum total of such practices constitutes the gospel order in its outward appearance for any particular generation. But since the social, political, economic, and religious factors of human life change from one historical period to another, it follows that the witness of God's people to the world in any particular age will vary according to the conditions of that age. Therefore, the gospel order will not have exactly the same outward manifestations in every age, but it will have the same center. Christ remains the same, the gospel remains the same, and the order of the gospel will remain the same, although its outward appearance may change in some particulars.

The Anabaptist and Quaker traditions remain the chief historical channels through which the vision of the disciple church has been transmitted to us. The Anabaptists and Quakers are the nearest approach to the disciple church since the Reformation; yet for three centuries they have traveled separate paths chiefly because of their differing approaches to the task of Christian renewal.

We may be thankful that they have shared the experience of witnessing and suffering for their Christian testimony against war and have had some measure of fellowship in that. But the world needs to be confronted now with a clear united call to the disciple church. This call is now being given with two voices. How can these two voices be brought into harmony at this critical point in the world's history?

Contemporary Responses

13

After Yoder

Failure, Authenticity, and the Renewal of the Mennonite Church

SUSANNE GUENTHER LOEWEN[1]

> Valuing conscientious objection to war does not mean we have not experienced other kinds of violence and warfare. John Howard Yoder is our collective, metaphorical unremoved shrapnel. How we remove it is just as important as understanding how the injury occurred and why we have lived with the embedded fragments for so long. —Malinda Berry[2]

In 2015, historian Rachel Waltner Goossen published "'Defanging the Beast': Mennonite Responses to John Howard Yoder's Sexual Abuse," a lengthy article commissioned by Mennonite Church USA and Anabaptist Mennonite Biblical Seminary (AMBS). Her findings shocked the Mennonite Church and academic community as she revealed that Yoder, credited with putting Mennonite peace theology on the map in ecumenical and academic circles, had sexually abused over 100 women over the course of his career.[3] The number of victims and the complicity of the church were devastating for many, as Malinda Berry's visceral language of "unremoved shrapnel"

---

1. Susanne Guenther Loewen is a pastor, theologian, and lecturer in Peace Studies in Saskatoon, Saskatchewan (Treaty 6 Territory and homeland of the Métis) where she lives with her spouse and two children. She holds a PhD in Mennonite and feminist nonviolent theologies of the cross from the Toronto School of Theology.

2. Berry, "Avoiding Avoidance."

3. See Waltner Goossen, "'Defanging the Beast,'" 7–80.

suggests. Others have described it similarly, given the profound dissonance of the most famous spokesperson of the historic peace church being a violent predator. Christian ethicist Karen Guth describes Yoder's abuses as causing "moral injury" to survivors, the Mennonite Church, and the Christian academy, on par with the effects of war on soldiers.[4] Mennonite historian Stephanie Krehbiel has similarly named the "multiple layers of spiritual carnage" surrounding sexual violence in the Mennonite Church, and Yoder's "haunting" the Mennonite Church even now, decades after his death.[5] These scholars suggest, with Berry, that Yoder's case indicates the wider failure of the Mennonite Church to respond to sexual abuse as a serious and pervasive peace issue.

In the wake of this failure, and in the era of #metoo and #churchtoo, marked by increased cultural awareness of sexual harassment and abuse, how does the Mennonite Church work toward ethical integrity in abuse response and prevention? How does it recover a sense of authenticity as a community striving to engage in ethical discernment and to embody justice and peace? In this chapter, I take the position that it is in facing and owning its failures—such as its (at best) inadequate response to Yoder's serial sexual abuses of women—that the Mennonite Church can experience renewal.[6] Though it may seem counterintuitive, it is in lamenting and addressing this failure that the Mennonite Church can begin to work toward integrity and authentic community—that is, a community that practices what it preaches and fosters honest self-reflection attuned to systemic power dynamics in its ethical discernment. In the Mennonite Church, this is work that has both begun and has yet to be completed, and work that, if done well, has the potential to renew the church. After defining postures that make space for authentic Christian community in conversation with the historic *Concern* articles, I will outline concrete practices that the academy and church can undertake as they work toward renewal, gleaned from various predominantly Mennonite and/or feminist theologians who have confronted the legacy of Yoder's sexual abuses. This task is made all the more urgent given that some of Yoder's writings are reprinted in this volume, and need to be engaged honestly, in light of his violence.

---

4. Guth, "Moral Injury," 167.
5. Krehbiel, "Pacifist Battlegrounds," 135, 138.
6. Lisa Schirch makes a similar argument in "To the Next Generation," 298–99. I am speaking here of Mennonite Church USA and my own denomination Mennonite Church Canada.

Hearing and Doing: Authenticity Then and Now

> [O]ne of our greatest needs [as the church] is the willingness to search constantly for authenticity in the Christian enterprise.[7]

Interestingly, the historical essays from *Concern* speak to the authenticity and integrity of the church—at times, using that very language. First published half a century ago, they reflect a common search for authentic community as a key aspect of the ongoing task of church renewal. In the wake of Yoder's abuses, our authenticity as a peace church—our ability to continue naming ourselves accurately as a peacemaking community with central values of lived discipleship, radical hospitality to the "least of these," and ethical discernment capable of addressing contemporary questions and issues—requires of us a sustained discussion around sexual abuse and the church as a particular instance of failure and opportunity for communal reflection and change. Three major characteristics of Mennonite theologies represented in the *Concern* essays create the conditions for such a discussion and thus begin to move us toward authenticity and church renewal.

1. A Concern for Authentic Discipleship and a Lived Christian Peace Ethic

Leland Harder follows J. Lawrence Burkholder in envisioning the congregation as "an ethical community, making ethical decisions and implementing them in the world," "like a local Peace Corps unit."[8] Relatedly, Virgil Vogt sees "'hearing' and 'doing'" or "revelation and response" as the twofold task of the church (Matt 7:24, Jas 1:23), asserting, "The revelation of God has no meaning for us until matched by our own response [and] . . . cooperation. 'Doing' is that process by which God's redemptive work becomes contemporary." He thereby calls for moving "beyond vague generalities" and "general principles" to "concrete situations."[9] These emphases on the church as a community of ethical discernment and lived, concrete faith make space for addressing real needs and particular situations of violence as a peace church.

---

7. Harder, "Changing Forms," essay in this volume, 81.
8. Burkholder quoted in Harder, "Changing Forms," essay in this volume, 90.
9. Vogt, "Small Congregations," essay in this volume, 53, 56. Cf. Miller, "Renewal," essay in this volume.

Vogt's language of "hearing and doing" is particularly poignant given the calls from Mennonite and/or feminist theologians to listen to the voices of victim-survivors of Yoder's sexual violence and take meaningful action in response. As Mennonite feminist theologian and AMBS professor Malinda Berry asserts, "Authentic reconciliation involves reparation, not just redemption. We often fasten our gaze on reconciliation and redemption, but I have learned that the humbling, and even humiliating, work of repairing the breach also has to be part of the equation lest we gloss over the depth of others' anger and rage."[10] Given the Mennonite Church and academy's "delayed response" to victim-survivor's experiences and warnings, peacebuilder Lisa Schirch calls for "action to make things right," including "victim-centered restorative justice" and the treatment of sexual violence as a peace issue.[11] As these comments suggest, the work of addressing concrete instances of violence is often more complex than abstract ideals around reconciliation. A recognition of the complexity of praxis as well as a reorientation toward a victim-centered, restorative justice approach have the potential to lead the church to a renewed sense of Christian discipleship and a more authentic communal peace ethic.

2. A Recognition of the Failures of the Church

In *Concern*, John W. Miller names the church "hypocritical," concerned with "hearing only" rather than "hearing and doing." Miller also faces the glaring failures of church history, noting that "Under the banner of Christianity fearful things have been and are being perpetrated. Under the banner of Christianity wars have been fought, slavery practiced, injustices defended, heretics killed and much more."[12] But others are not as forthright concerning the church's ethical failures. Paul Miller speaks pejoratively of "sub-Christian society," and Yoder makes overstated claims about the fidelity of Anabaptism to the New Testament church[13]—a stance which "turns an opportunity for self-reflection into a way to scapegoat foreign influences," according to

---

10. Berry, "Avoiding Avoidance."

11. Schirch, "To the Next Generation," 285, 299, 294–95. Cf. Scarsella and Krehbiel, "Sexual Violence," 10.

12. Miller, "Renewal," essay in this volume, 97.

13. Miller, "Can the Adult Sunday School," essay in this volume, 35; Yoder, "Marginalia (excerpt, 1960)," essay in this volume, 5; Cf. Scarsella's discussion of Yoder's intolerance of theological diversity in "Not Making Sense."

Mennonite pastor and theologian Isaac Villegas.[14] This kind of triumphalism and self-righteousness gets in the way of an honest reading of church history, including recent Mennonite Church history.

Canadian Mennonite theologian Jeremy Bergen discusses this dynamic in reference to church apologies wherein the church "essentially expresses regret over a state of affairs but is evasive about its own agency" or responsibility, or when a church uses its apology to claim it has earned forgiveness and a "singular . . . moral credibility." Bergen continues, "This may exhibit precisely the ecclesial triumphalism that is at the root in many histories the churches now seek to disavow."[15] By contrast, Berry and Schirch call for the church to "be honest about Yoder's failings," to face and name the church's failure to respond adequately to victim-survivors of his abuses, and to focus on lament and healing as the path to "recovering integrity."[16] In Bergen's view, this requires the church to make itself "vulnerable to the judgment of the wronged other . . . over an undetermined time" as a "form of penance."[17] As in Truth and Reconciliation Commissions, this vulnerable, victim-centered posture makes space for the clear naming of wrongdoing and harm, which is a necessary precursor to "promoting . . . a new culture and commitment to a shared future."[18] With this appropriate attention to lament, honest self-reflection and facing of failure, renewal and healing begin to become possibilities for the church.

3. A Willingness to Engage the Contemporary Context

Alongside a recognition of the failures of the church comes an openness to difficult contemporary questions facing the church. Lewis Benson speaks helpfully of the Quaker understanding of Christ not primarily as a historical figure, but as a living Presence experienced by the church today. "Quakerism is not a new attempt to apply the principles of that Reformation that was begun in the sixteenth century. . . . It can only rightly be understood in terms of a new departure in the story of Christian renewal."[19]

---

14. Villegas, "Ecclesial Ethics," 13.

15. Bergen, "Whether, and How," 135, 139. There remains a subtle othering of victim-survivors in this perspective, however, as they are not seen as representing "the church."

16. Berry, "Avoiding Avoidance," and Schirch, "To the Next Generation," 287.

17. Bergen, "Whether, and How," 145.

18. Chapman, "Truth Commissions," 258.

19. Benson, "Order," essay in this volume, 124. This contradicts Yoder's emphasis on

This awareness of contemporary questions makes space for conversation around the #metoo and #churchtoo movements, as well as emerging academic fields of trauma theology and feminist, womanist, and queer theologies that centralize gendered, historically marginalized experiences, including experiences of sexual violence.[20] These new theologies confirm and expand Hans-Ruedi Weber's notion that "we can become ourselves (i.e., real human beings, children of God) only through the other"—that is, only in relationship.[21] In conversation with these new streams of theology, we might add it is only through listening to those who have historically been "othered"—including victim-survivors of sexual violence—that the church becomes an authentic Christian community with ethical integrity. Such a community displays a radical sense of hospitality toward the "least of these" (Matt 25) that takes intentional steps to dismantle hierarchical understandings of power in Jesus's way of peace with justice.

On the Way: Steps toward Integrity and Peace

> As AMBS's current president . . . I confess that this seminary failed in our use of the power entrusted to us. . . . Enamored by the brilliance that put our treasured peace theology on the world stage, we failed to truly listen to those whose bodies, minds, and spirits were being crushed. . . . There is no excuse when a theological school that is dedicated to teach what is good and true and beautiful about the gospel, fails in a most egregious way to comfort those who mourn, to bring good news to the oppressed, to bind up the broken hearted, and proclaim liberty to the captives. . . . We failed you.[22]

Shortly after Waltner Goossen's article was published, Anabaptist Mennonite Biblical Seminary, where Yoder had taught and abused people, held a Service of Lament, Confession, and Commitment. This service, including Sara Wenger Shenk's apology, came to symbolize a turning point in the

---

obedience to biblical authority and the New Testament church, as well as denigration of human responsibility in Yoder, "Marginalia (excerpt, 1960)," and Yoder, "Marginalia: A Syllabus of Issues," essays in this volume.

20. See Scarsella and Krehbiel, "Sexual Violence," 8–9, and Scarsella, "Not Making Sense." Cf. Berry, "Avoiding Avoidance."

21. Weber, "Church in the House," essay in this volume, 16.

22. Wenger Shenk, "Statement of Confession."

Mennonite institutional response to Yoder's sexual abuses.²³ After decades of "the church's denial and secrecy about who [Yoder] really was," including the sealing of documents at his request, here was a process involving the seminary president as well as Mennonite Church USA leader Ervin Stutzman and four Mennonite sexual violence experts. Begun at the request of mental health worker Carolyn Holderread Heggen, a survivor of Yoder's sexual harassment who had led efforts to hold him accountable for years, this process took seriously her conviction that the church "would never be vital again until this issue was addressed."²⁴ Shenk's apology has been praised for its "transparency," its clear admission of failure, and its centering and validating of the experiences and pain of victim-survivors of Yoder's abuses,²⁵ all of which provide glimmers of hope for the revitalization and renewal of the church as an authentic community of ethical integrity. In this apology, we see real steps taken toward the vitality of the church. In the final section below, I name other concrete ways the Mennonite academy and church can build on the momentum of this apology to deal more adequately with Yoder's legacy for the sake of a more holistic and inclusive peace theology and ecclesiology.

Mennonite Peace Theology and Ethics

For some time now, Mennonite feminists have identified patterns of male domination in the Mennonite theological academy as both enabling Yoder's abuse and resulting from it, since he targeted women students who showed leadership skills, driving many of them out of the Mennonite academy.²⁶ Schirch observes, "The continuing absence of women in many centers of pacifist theology at Mennonite institutions today means that new generations of pacifist theologians may also not be informed by a gender or power analysis to take into consideration the privilege and entitlement that males enjoy."²⁷ One example is the ongoing refusal among some Yoderian theo-

---

23. Waltner Goossen, "Mennonite Bodies, Sexual Ethics," 248–55.

24. Krehbiel, "Pacifist Battlegrounds," 150–51.

25. Waltner Goossen, "Mennonite Bodies, Sexual Ethics," 255. Cf. Bergen, "Whether, and How," 145.

26. Schirch, "To the Next Generation," 286. Cf. Waltner Goossen, "Mennonite Bodies, Sexual Ethics," 254.

27. Schirch, "To the Next Generation," 292.

logians to engage feminist—or even female—scholars,[28] including Stanley Hauerwas, who has recently reiterated that he is not "prepared to discuss feminist theology" while insisting that women should be reading Yoder's work.[29] Ruth Krall, longtime advocate for Yoder's victim-survivors in the Mennonite Church, speaks of similarly dismissive attitudes in that since the 1970s, the "work of advocate women has been seen and named as gossip, rumor, and innuendo rather than as a contribution to Yoder scholarship."[30] This imbalance has been exacerbated by sexual violence not being seen as a "real" peace issue by many male peace theologians, despite Mennonite feminist theologians calling for reflection on sexual violence from peace church perspectives since at least 1992.[31] Many male peace theologians, including Yoder, have minimized the seriousness of sexual assault and abuse, deeming it less important than the violence of poverty or war, and suggesting, in Krehbiel's words, that "real violence happens elsewhere."[32]

Much remains to be done to address the gender imbalance in Mennonite academic circles and beyond, including working for equity in representation ("women's presence and flourishing")[33] in academic institutions, becoming informed about patterns and language around the trauma of sexual abuse, and committing to support victim-survivors of Yoder's and other abusers.[34] Here, again, AMBS has paved the way in working with Into

28. As Malinda Berry wonders, "Why don't more of my men colleagues engage feminist theology and the women who develop it? I pose this question here because there are both feminist theologians and scholars within the Mennonite sphere and because there are feminist theologians and scholars beyond our immediate sphere and conversations all who care deeply about social change and transformation." See Berry, "Yoderian Messianism." Cf. Guth, "Doing Justice," 131.

29. Quoted in Scarsella, "Not Making Sense."

30. Krall, "Writer's Voice," 13.

31. Yoder, *Peace Theology*. Lydia Neufeld Harder points out that Carol Penner is the only contributor to this volume who overtly critiques Yoder's theology. See Neufeld Harder, *Challenge*, 66–67.

32. Krehbiel, "Pacifist Battlegrounds," 142–43, 168. Much of this minimization is reflected in language of "dalliances," "affairs," or "experiments" rather than naming Yoder's actions as sexual abuse, violence, or violation, as well as in language of "allegations" or "accusations," used long after the events had been investigated and proven, and even Yoder himself had admitted the truth of the events. See Krall, "Tales from the Reptile House," 153–54. Carol Penner also notes that Yoder minimizes sexual assault in his book, *What Would You Do?*, claiming it is "an irrelevant emotional element which clouds a rational discussion of assault." See Penner, "Content to Suffer," 106.

33. Guth, "Doing Justice," 132.

34. Based on Schirch, "To the Next Generation," 299–300.

Account, a survivor advocate group, to address its mishandling of a recent student's sexual assault.[35] The process of theological renewal has already begun in the recognition among many Mennonite theologians that on its own, Yoder's work is an inadequate representation of Mennonite peace theology. Berry has argued that "our ecclesial community has been too reliant on John Howard Yoder for our theological perspective. . . . My view is that, alone, Yoder's work does not offer us a sufficient analysis of power that helps us understand what is happening theologically in faith communities where we perpetuate cycles of violence and injustice."[36] Trauma theologian Hilary Scarsella agrees, asserting, "feminist thought offers precisely the tools that Hauerwas [and other peace theologians] would have needed in order to avoid promoting logics that sustain sexual violence"[37]—such as clarifying the "integral role that sexualized violence plays in war,"[38] and the patterns of sexual predators, such as Yoder positioning himself as friendly to feminists,[39] which Krehbiel argues was a grooming tactic.[40] In applying intersectional feminist, queer, and trauma-informed theological insights and power analyses to Mennonite peace theologies, as Mennonite feminists have already been doing, a more authentic peace theology and ethics emerges. This integrated approach leads to redefining violence beyond militarism to encompass intersectional forms of systemic violence, including sexual violation and gender-based violence. Correspondingly, peace ethics are broadened beyond nonresistance to reflect the work of nonviolent resistance to systemic forms of violence, informed by multiple voices and

---

35. See Wenger Shenk, "AMBS Response to Victims," and Scarsella, "Hope and the Work."

36. Berry, "Avoiding Avoidance." Cf. Schirch, "To the Next Generation," 293, and Scarsella, "Not Making Sense." Scarsella views Yoder's "lack of sustained critical engagement with feminism, womanism, black theology, liberation theology, and queer theology" as proof that "Yoder's theology has not proved necessary (or even useful) for theology interested in dismantling the powers of whiteness, patriarchal gender constructions, or rape culture." Scarsella and Krehbiel, "Sexual Violence," 8, also state, "We do not agree with [Mennonite Church publisher] Herald that Yoder deserves to be heard."

37. Scarsella, "Not Making Sense," and Krehbiel, "Pacifist Battlegrounds," 147–48. Cf. Schirch, "To the Next Generation," 288–9.

38. Krehbiel, "Pacifist Battlegrounds," 147–48. Cf. Schirch, "To the Next Generation," 288–89, 294–95.

39. Guth, "Doing Justice," 122, 126. She argues that peace or "witness" theologians should engage feminists because Yoder himself valued their contributions to theology, but such an argument ignores patterns of sexual predation and grooming.

40. Krehbiel, "Pacifist Battlegrounds," 152–53.

gendered experiences within and beyond the church.[41] Along these lines, Guth calls for a recognition of "those courageous and principled women who stood up, decried the abuse, and insisted on setting wrongs right" as nonviolent witnesses.[42] Together with the next generation(s) of Mennonite feminist theologians who have critiqued Yoder, these women have acted as "conscientious objectors"[43] to sexual violence, often at a personal cost,[44] as they seek a more holistic view of peace. In fostering trauma-informed and gender-egalitarian institutional cultures in the Mennonite academy as well as recognizing Mennonite feminist contributions to peace theologies and practice, we begin to see evidence of a shift with transformative possibilities for the renewal of the Mennonite academy and theology.

Mennonite Peace Ecclesiology

According to Schirch, "despite previous efforts by church leaders to stop [Yoder's] abuse and to enable healing, further work on the part of the church is being called for and is indeed needed."[45] The initial church disciplinary process from 1992–96 resulted in the permanent suspension of Yoder's ministerial credentials, but the Indiana-Michigan Mennonite Conference concluded it by thanking Yoder for his cooperation and recommending the continued use of "his gifts of writing and teaching."[46] Many

41. "Trauma awareness should not be treated as an additive, but rather as a theological responsibility that will disrupt and transform core beliefs that exacerbate sexual violence, and push toward greater engagement with the systemic inequities in which Christianity has been complicit." See Scarsella and Krehbiel, "Sexual Violence," 9.

42. Guth, "Doing Justice," 121, 131–32. This would include Carolyn Holderread Heggen, Ruth Krall, Barbra Graber, Lydia Neufeld Harder, Martha Smith Good, Carol Penner. Cf. Waltner Goossen, "Mennonite Bodies, Sexual Ethics," 251–55.

43. Penner, "Mennonite Silences," 174, 171. Newer voices critiquing Yoder would include Malinda Berry, Lisa Schirch, Hilary Scarsella, Isaac Villegas, David Cramer, Stephanie Krehbiel, Hannah Heinzekehr, Kimberly Penner, and myself.

44. Krall, "Writer's Voice," 14–15, where she states, "I noticed, and so did many other women, that the AMBS March 22, 2015 service of confession and lament vis-à-vis the seminary's historical mismanagement of John Howard Yoder's sexual abuses, was largely a female confession and lament. Two women carried the seminary's historical burden of responsibility for confession. . . . I conclude, therefore, that academic Mennonite men, in general, do not see sexual violence as an important peace and justice issue. They most certainly do not risk their careers to support the victims of violence. While there are exceptions to this, they are rare."

45. Schirch, "To the Next Generation," 286.

46. Krehbiel, "Pacifist Battlegrounds," 163. Krehbiel notes that while Yoder's

were profoundly disappointed by the lack of attention to victim-survivors[47] and the lack of transparency surrounding Yoder's resistance to the process and refusal to apply his own teachings on accountability to himself.[48] Villegas has pointed out that during the time of this disciplinary action, Yoder altered his theology of church discipline based on Matthew 18 in "self-serving" ways that centered the offender's restoration to the community and sidelined the needs of victims.[49]

AMBS's apology sets the tone for a new approach, but more remains to be done in equipping Mennonite congregations to prevent and respond well to sexual violence. Krall observes that the decade following public revelations of Yoder's abuses saw significant awareness-raising around sexual abuse within Mennonite communities, much of it led by Mennonite Central Committee (MCC),[50] which continues to provide resources today.[51] But because of the congregational polity of the Mennonite Church, application remains inconsistent. Speaking for my own context of Mennonite Church Saskatchewan, we do not have an MCC Abuse Response and Prevention Office like Manitoba and British Columbia, yet there is momentum around restorative justice programs like Circles of Support and Accountability, which provides community to convicted sexual abusers. While these efforts laudably prevent recidivism and restore dignity to offenders,[52] it is deeply problematic that there are no comparable supports for victim-survivors. At least implicitly, Yoder's overemphasis on the offender's needs and sidelining of victims has remained influential. In response, a group of church leaders (a counselor, restorative justice practitioners, a camp worker, and theologians, including myself) are working to broaden pastors' and congregations' understandings and practices of restorative justice and peacemaking to include the needs of victim-survivors of sexual violence. We are calling ourselves Safe Church Too—a reference to Safe Church policies meant to educate and prevent sexual abuse in the church and the #churchtoo movement, which

---

"ministerial license was revoked and never restored," that sanction was somewhat meaningless since, "as a career academic, he had little use for it anyway."

47. Waltner Goossen, "Mennonite Bodies, Sexual Ethics," 248–49.
48. See Cramer et al., "Theology and Misconduct."
49. See Villegas, "Ecclesial Ethics," 15–17.
50. Krall, "Tales from the Reptile House," 143.
51. See MCC Canada's abuse response and prevention website at https://abuseresponseandprevention.ca/. Carol Penner has provided a lot of leadership around these resources in Mennonite Church Canada.
52. See Circles of Support and Accountability Canada.

makes space to name experiences of sexual abuse in the church. In focusing on the specific needs of victim-survivors alongside the needs of offenders, a more inclusive and holistic peacebuilding practice begins to emerge, with great potential to bring healing to the church.

Finally, work remains to be done in revising our spirituality and worship, which reflects an overemphasis on self-abnegation. This dynamic—present in everything from Lent and Easter sermons, understandings of the cross, salvation, redemptive suffering, and practices of Communion[53]—reflects the ongoing influence of peace understood as "nonresistance"[54] and Yoder's notions of "revolutionary subordination," which Mennonite feminists have been denouncing for decades.[55] Mennonite women especially are working to remedy this truncated version of the gospel that downplays a spirituality of empowerment and responsibility.[56] Scarsella, for instance, has worked with others to revise the Communion liturgy with sensitivity to survivors of sexual violence, including such lines as, "We flourish in your love, as we express your love among ourselves and with our neighbors. We find safety and peace in the beloved community of faith."[57] Trauma and feminist theologies can, in this way, be incorporated into our very liturgies and worship practices, emphasizing the needs of victim-survivors—empowerment, safety, healing, and peace—in every part of the life of the Mennonite Church.

As the historic *Concern* articles recognized, the search for authentic community and the task of church renewal are ongoing—there are always new questions of discipleship to discern, new failures with which to grapple, new contemporary issues to address in our context. The recovery of ethical integrity and the healing of the wounds of John Howard Yoder's sexual abuses in and beyond the Mennonite peace church will likewise take time and sustained effort—this is no linear process to a quick reconciliation.

---

53. For a helpful review, see Scarsella and Krehbiel, "Sexual Violence," 3–5. Cf. Susanne Guenther Loewen, "Can the Cross," 109–21.

54. This is still the definition in the official statement of shared beliefs: See article 22 in the *Confession of Faith in a Mennonite Perspective*. Krall notes how this is especially inadequate and harmful in perpetuating cycles of sexual abuse: Krall, "Living Inside," 105.

55. See Penner, "Content to Suffer," 103–4, and Schirch, "To the Next Generation," 290–1. Cf. Scarsella, "Not Making Sense."

56. See Castro, *I've Got the Power*. There is sadly no official Mennonite Church Canada version of the Women in Leadership Project, which treats sexism as a peace issue.

57. See Scarsella et al., "Lord's Supper" 33–48. Cf. Jones, *Trauma and Grace*.

Still, in the theologies and witness of the theologians, peacebuilders, pastors, historians, and communities cited here, many of them Mennonite and/or feminist, this work has already begun. The "shrapnel" Berry spoke of has begun to be removed. This work grounds hope for many as it makes its way into the lived theology of the church, shaping and equipping the Mennonite Church into a community of hearing and doing, a community of authenticity and integrity, a community embodying a holistic and just peace. These are the roots of renewal that have the potential to carry the Mennonite Church and academy beyond Yoder's violent legacy into a renewed calling to be people of God's healing and peace.

14

A Global Communion as a Condition for the Possibility of Church Renewal

César García[1]

Introduction

Do you consider Mennonite World Conference (MWC) a global communion? That was the question that a leader from a hierarchical church tradition asked me with surprise. From her perspective, the emphasis that many Anabaptist-Mennonites give to the local congregation in their ecclesiology is not coherent with the idea of a structure that goes beyond a local body and that at the same time is considered a church, in this case a *global* church.

"Yes, MWC is called to be a global communion," I responded. "Today MWC brings together 10,000 congregations distributed in 107 national churches, plus many entities that are an expression of those churches in the Anabaptist tradition. My call as General Secretary of MWC is to nurture that communion." In this essay, based on my years of service with MWC, I reflect on how a global communion can be conceived from an Anabaptist point of view and why a global perspective is important in our ecclesiology today.

The task of imagining global church, while not unique to Anabaptists, takes on a particular shape in a tradition marked by Believers' Church

---

1. César García is general secretary of Mennonite World Conference (MWC), an organization that serves some 1.5 million members around the world in the Anabaptist tradition. García is from Bogotá, Colombia. He has been a church planter, pastor, and professor of Bible and theology.

ecclesiology and strong local autonomy. Understanding ourselves as a global communion is one of the challenges that we face in some regions of the Mennonite world. The question of the need for a global communion is often raised in Canadian and United States (US) Anabaptist settings. In contrast, in contexts of persecution, oppression, or violence, reasons why we need a global church seem more evident to our members, and more pragmatic: a global communion offers the support (e.g., financial resources, political advocacy, pastoral care) that local congregations and regional churches need in order to cope with difficult circumstances. In the Majority World, global interdependency is crucial for projects that surpass the capacity of a local or regional church (e.g., missions, theological education, formation of new agencies).

On the other hand, in Canadian and US Anabaptist contexts, the idea of a church that goes beyond the local congregation is often rejected. "We do not have a pope" is a common saying among us. However, it seems that in practice Anabaptists have thousands of popes, each exercising authority over a local congregation or a conference. Many are not accountable to others because of the lack of structures that facilitate such accountability. Abuse and centralization of power in top-down structures have pushed some Anabaptists to lose trust in ecclesial entities bigger than a local congregation. Part of this tendency is evident in the writings of the *Concern* pamphlet series.

In addition to the abuse of power identified as a church problem in the fifties and sixties, today I would add increasing racism, nationalism, and fragmentation to the list of weaknesses among us. Renewal, as an ongoing biblical invitation (Rom 12:1–2), demands a response to these realities. The global church is stronger when it has some sort of organic structure that overcomes nationalism and facilitates mutual accountability without authoritarian leadership. A global *communion* provides the possibility of such renewal by fostering unity, interdependency, and transnational Christ-center identity. A cross-cultural global communion allows us to live out the messianic vision of new relations in which we face and address economic inequities and systems of racialized domination.

New Testament *Ecclesia*

Concern articles rightly identify the house church structure as a path to Christian renewal. Local congregations and house churches facilitate communities of discipleship—small groups of Christians that meet informally for Bible study, prayer, and worship. *Concern* critiques a wrong use of centralized power and the burden of an over-institutionalized church. However, an immediate question emerges. If we insist on authority resting in the local congregation, why stop with the congregation when we push discernment, decision-making, and power downward? Why not place such authority in the individual believer? The authors of *Concern* respond that the New Testament speaks of the interdependency of individuals in the context of a local congregation or house church.

Nevertheless, the New Testament does not give the picture of lonely, independent, and individualistic house churches. Our Anabaptist tradition needs to recover the idea of regional churches and a visible global church. We need to work on what might be named Anabaptist catholicity—a universal church from an Anabaptist perspective. The reason I affirm this has to do with the New Testament concept and practice of *ecclesia*. Scriptures speak of interdependent local congregations that lean on each other for theology, pastoral care, financial support in times of crisis, and mission, among other things.

As an example, we can point to the way the New Testament is structured. There are four Gospels that speak about Jesus. Each reflects the experience of its author with Jesus Christ. Each grows out of an oral tradition that reflects the wisdom of different communities. These theological writings do not show Jesus in exactly the same way. There is a great deal of diversity among them. Why do we not have just one Gospel, the fruit of only one local congregation? Why do we need four different points of view that give different understandings about Jesus?

From its beginning, the church saw unity in such diversity as something crucial, something that could help followers of Jesus better understand who Jesus is. An interdependent testimony about Jesus, kept and shaped by several different communities, gives us a fuller picture of the meaning of following Christ than we could get from one uniform account about Jesus. The apostolic church did not use the experience of one community (e.g., Jerusalem) as the only perspective it needed to be taking into account. From the beginning, the testimony about Jesus was interdependent and validated by several communities together. We need diversity and multiple congregations in order to know Jesus better.

Another example relates to the Council of Jerusalem. In Acts 15 we have the account of several local congregations and regions with *deep* disagreements. Their representatives arrived from different cities and cultures in order to deal with their theological and ethical differences. It seems that diversity and even discrepancies are necessary in the body of Christ if we want to know the meaning of communal unity, communal love, communal forgiveness, communal patience, and communal self-denial. It is important to highlight that in this passage we do not see local congregations being allowed to decide by themselves on the acceptance or rejection of gentiles as members of the church. This was a theological issue with multiple ethical implications. Experience, biblical interpretation, and tradition all were at stake. The book of Acts illustrates that some issues require a *trans-local, cross-cultural decision-making* structure that moves the whole church toward consensus. Sometimes, this is essential for hearing God's voice about specific matters (Acts 15:28).

Following this pattern, in letters of the apostle Paul, we learn that in the midst of disagreements local congregations were not expected to act by themselves. *Independent* house churches is not a valid New Testament option. Disagreements sometimes may cause us to distance ourselves from brothers and sisters (Acts 15:39). However, that is different from starting new, separated, and disconnected churches. Divisions in the body of Christ are not always the result of faithfulness but can emerge from sinful attitudes and bad conflict management (Eph 4).

We see how in the book of Ephesians—the most complete treatment on ecclesiology in the New Testament—the church is understood as a unified people, made up from diverse social fragments and cultures. Such unity is possible only because of the work of the Holy Spirit,[2] when Jesus constitutes the center and new identity of those fragments. In this new people, a new kind of interdependent and loving relationship replaces nationalism, racism, and other idolatrous allegiances.

Church as Alternative Global Communion

The Ephesian model understands the church as an alternative community that transcends a geographic localized cultural expression. This model includes people from many congregations in many nations. Such an

2. According to Ephesians, that unity in the body of Christ is a *gift* to be enjoyed. It is not a human endeavor. It is not the result of agreement on doctrinal matters, racial or social homogeneity, common foundational narratives, or a shared vision. Unity is a miracle of the Holy Spirit that we may receive and live out in the midst of theological, cultural and social diversity.

alternative global community counters injustice by its very existence. The church does so by living out a new kingdom of love and bringing hope when it shows that a new and different society is possible when dependent on God. "This church knows that its most credible form of witness (and the most 'effective' thing it can do for the world) is the actual creation of a living, breathing, visible community of faith,"[3] affirms Protestant theologian Stanley Hauerwas.

It is only in a global communion that structural economic inequalities and racial systems of domination may be overcome. It is through our way of living as a just, multicultural family of faith that unjust powers of this world such as nationalism, ethnocentrism, and indifference are exposed. In the words of biblical scholar Walter Wink, "exposing the delusional system is the central ascetical task in our discernment of the Powers. For the Powers are never more powerful than when they can act from concealment."[4] Individualism, nationalism, and consumerism are some of the false gods that offer to individuals a reason for living today but at the same time provide excuses to oppress other societies. Only a multicultural global family of faith that loves each other, overcomes nationalism, and looks out for the wellbeing of others will bring a new standard that exposes the delusional values of our world.

Mennonite theologian John Driver says that God's reign is made manifest through the concrete forms that life takes on among God's people, and it is precisely in the midst of relationships among them that the perfect kingdom becomes a reality.[5] It follows that a kingdom that involves people from every tribe and nation is evidenced only in concrete, visible relationships. Those relationships in God's kingdom are of love and not of domination. They are made possible by a new identity in Christ that facilitates the overcoming of racism and ethnocentrism. In the words of Catholic theologian Gerhard Lohfink, "the real being of Christ can be bright only if the church makes visible the messianic alternative and the new eschatological creation that happens from Christ."[6] Without a visible global communion or church, the kind of renewal that exposes sinful loyalties to human kingdoms is not possible.

---

3. Hauerwas and Willimon, *Resident Aliens*, 47.
4. Wink, *Engaging the Powers*, 88.
5. Cf. Driver, "Kingdom of God," 86.
6. Lohfink, *La Iglesia*, 191–92, author's translation.

Concern critique of the existence of Anabaptist church institutions that go beyond the local congregation was initially focused on the centralization of power.[7] It was related to the hierarchical leadership style that was present in Mennonite Central Committee and other Mennonite organizations at that time.[8] But the problem does not have to do with the creation of institutions. It has to do with the way some of them emerged in Anabaptist history: from divisions and fragmentation, duplicating efforts and competing among each other, privileging bureaucracy and hierarchical leadership styles, and in many cases struggling with the survival of oversized structures.

Anabaptist Catholicity

Concern pamphlets help us imagine (by contrast) appropriate structures and institutional forms that a global communion must have in the Anabaptist tradition. The entire fifth issue of Concern (1958), for example, was dedicated to the idea of the house church structure as a paradigm of the Early Church. The articles suggest characteristics that may be built up in a regional or global church: being active in witness and service, centering on relationships, seeking to keep unity in Christ, and fostering interdependency.[9]

Hans-Ruedi Weber points out that a regional manifestation of the church cannot be a conglomeration of individuals or a federation of church organizations. It must be an organic union of local congregations.[10] Those that object to "institutionalism" are really calling for more organic, more accessible, more accountable institutions. In contrast to social organizations based on domination, exploitation, accumulation, and force, a global church in the Anabaptist tradition can live as a transnational people, being a cross-cultural diaspora in constant exile. It must be relational and centered on people, instead of focusing on the survival of its own structure.

---

7. See essays in this volume: Weber, "Church in the House"; Miller, "Can the Adult Sunday School"; Studer, "Evangelism"; Vogt, "Small Congregations"; Yoder, "Marginalia (excerpt, 1960)."

8. Cf. Hershberger, "Power, Tradition, and Renewal," 157–59.

9. See for example Vogt, "Small Congregations," essay in this volume.

10. Weber, "Church in the House," essay in this volume.

A Global Communion as Transnational Citizenship

By a global transnational citizenship people, I mean the kind of community in which identity is not based on race, nationality, financial capacity, or political borders. As a transnational and cross-cultural diaspora, identity is based on the centrality of Christ. Therefore:

- Its structure will resist the human tendency of domination and inequality. It will do so by privileging horizontal leadership patterns over top-down authority. Decisions will be made by consensus instead of by simple majority. Each church will contribute in an environment of equality and mutual respect regardless of its racial background, number of members, or financial and academic capacity. Positions of service will be determined by looking for a balance which takes into account cultural, gender, and social location of the candidates—gifts that the Holy Spirit has given to God's people.

- Its structure will be organized and managed taking into account the way in which the church expresses itself in each context instead of imposing monocultural paradigms. Issues that are discussed will never be the result of imposition or manipulation. Management styles will apply models and concepts from several cultures while respecting differences and contrasting points of view.

- Its structure will not look for uniformity. Due to the fact that all persons and congregations are respected equally, while particular gifts and expertise organize collective activity appropriately for the benefit of all, diversity will be celebrated and encouraged.

A Global Communion as a Relational, Organic Structure

A global church in the Anabaptist tradition must be an *organic community* and not a *bureaucratic institution*. This means that it exists to serve people and churches, not to build infrastructure simply for its own survival. The structure should be easy to adapt and modify in order to facilitate fulfillment of its call, and its budget should evidence priorities and values that are consistent with it.

Even though it is important to have strong and healthy bodies that follow organizational plans, policies, and principles, this should not be done at the expense of the people the structure serves. The administrative focus of ecclesial entities that go beyond local congregations must be primarily *pastoral*. A pastoral focus will promote symmetrical and reciprocal relationships among congregations and conferences. It will develop vulnerable leadership that facilitates interdependency. Because relations (being one in Christ) are more important than structures:

- agencies that belong to a global communion will develop their ministry without competing with each other.
- initiatives of local congregations or conferences will be born in mutual consultation and will avoid attitudes that promote fragmentation or independency.

This understanding of a global church may imply that some structures in our Anabaptist Church must disappear for the sake of unity. There are too many institutions and agencies that compete with each other. There are too many regional and national conferences that work independently or are a result of a division that does not make sense anymore. There is too much institutional weight that makes us slow in accomplishing our mission. There is duplication of efforts, and in some places too many leaders that are not accountable to others and exercise an authoritarian leadership style. I agree with *Concern* about the need for change, but the way to renewal does not end with reducing the church to a group of independent local congregations.

Conclusion

Participating in a global church offers opportunities to experience a kind of transnational citizenship that allows the global church to embody an alternative to the violent, nationalistic, and divisive politics of today's empires. Escaping from nationalist idolatry means being church globally, experiencing a new creation and a new political reality. That reality, from an Anabaptist perspective, will promote light and adaptable structures, focused on relationships, and with a pastoral leadership of humble service. Our world needs to see an Anabaptist catholicity lived out today. That is our vision and invitation in MWC.

MWC started around one hundred years ago as a response to racism, nationalism, violence, and persecution in Europe. During the last fifty years its leaders have developed a vision and theological framework that call us to become a global communion in the Anabaptist tradition. Its structure facilitates the participation of members in a cross-cultural way. It encourages decision-making processes where all can participate regardless of the number of members of the national church that they represent and regardless financial capacity or academic training.

MWC does not own buildings or have a bureaucratic structure to preserve. In an organic way it facilitates our communion by focusing on relations and interdependency. It challenges nationalism by affirming a cross-cultural common identity in Christ. It confronts racism by celebrating cultural diversity and affirming a variety of worship styles, theologies, and ways of being church. It helps us walk together in suffering and joy, poverty and abundance, persecution and freedom.

We are on the way to becoming a global communion that practices many of the principles outlined in this article. We have not arrived yet, which is precisely what renewal is: an ongoing process until all of us "come to the unity of the faith and of the knowledge of the Son of God, to maturity, to the measure of the full stature of Christ" (Eph 4:13). Let's walk together so that, in Jesus's words, the world may believe (John 17:21).

APPENDIX

Concern Republication Volumes

The original Concern pamphlet series consisted of eighteen volumes that were published between 1954 and 1971. What follows in this index is a complete listing of that content as reorganized in the seven-volume series published by Wipf and Stock.

The Roots of Concern: *Writings on Anabaptist Renewal 1952–1957*, ed. Virgil Vogt. Eugene, OR: Wipf & Stock, 2009.

Concern *for Education: Essays on Christian Higher Education, 1958–1966*, ed. Virgil Vogt. Eugene, OR: Wipf & Stock, 2010.

Concern *for the Church in the World: Essays on Christian Responsibility, 1958–1963*, ed. Laura Schmidt Roberts. Eugene, OR: Wipf & Stock, 2022.

Concern *for Church Renewal: Essays on Community and Discipleship, 1958–1966*, ed. Laura Schmidt Roberts. Eugene, OR: Wipf & Stock, 2022.

Concern *for Church Mission and Spiritual Gifts: Essays on Faith and Culture, 1958–1968*, ed. Laura Schmidt Roberts. Eugene, OR: Wipf & Stock, 2022.

Concern *for Church Polity and Discipline: Essays on Pastoral Ministry and Communal Authority, 1958–1969*, ed. Laura Schmidt Roberts. Eugene, OR: Wipf & Stock, 2022.

APPENDIX: *CONCERN* REPUBLICATION VOLUMES

CONCERN *for Anabaptist Renewal: A Radical Reformation Reader, 1971*, ed. Virgil Vogt and Laura Schmidt Roberts. Eugene, OR: Wipf & Stock, 2022.

***The Roots of* CONCERN: *Writings on Anabaptist Renewal 1952–1957*,** ed. Virgil Vogt. Eugene, OR: Wipf & Stock, 2009.

   Virgil Vogt, "Foreword"

   Paul Peachey, "The Historical Genesis of the CONCERN Project"

   The Original Frontispiece of CONCERN Volumes 1–4

CONCERN 1 (1954)

   Paul Peachey, "Introduction"

   Paul Peachey, "Toward an Understanding of the Decline of the West"

   John Howard Yoder, "The Anabaptist Dissent: The Logic of the Place of the Disciple in Society"

CONCERN 2 (1955)

   Paul Peachey, "Preface"

   John W. Miller, "The Church in the Old Testament"

   Paul Peachey, "Spirit and Form in the Church of Christ"

   David A. Shank and John Howard Yoder, "Biblicism and the Church"

   Appendix: "Close communion—On what lines?"

CONCERN 3 (1956)

   Paul Peachey, "Preface"

   C. Norman Kraus and John W. Miller, "Intimations of Another Way: A Progress Report"

   Hans-Joachim Wiehler, "Preaching in the Church?"

   J. Lester Brubaker and Sol Yoder, "A CONCERN Retreat [CONCERN and Camp Luz]"

   Lewis Benson, "The Call: Journal of Spiritual Reformation"

   Notes on books

APPENDIX: *CONCERN* REPUBLICATION VOLUMES

Concern 4 (June 1957)

    Paul Peachey, "Preface"

    "Epistolary: An Exchange by Letter"

    Paul Peachey, "What Is Concern?"

    John Howard Yoder, "What Are Our Concerns?"

    John W. Miller, "Organization and Church"

    Herbert Klassen, "Property: A Problem in Christian Ethics"

Concern *for Education: Essays on Christian Higher Education, 1958–1966*, ed. Virgil Vogt. Eugene, OR: Wipf & Stock, 2010.

    Virgil Vogt, "Editor's Note"

    Michael Cartwright, "Foreword"

    John Howard Yoder, "Christian Education: Doctrinal Orientation" (1959)

    John Howard Yoder, "A Syllabus of Issues Facing the Church College" (1964)

    John Howard Yoder and Paul M. Lederach, "Theological Statements for a Philosophy of Mennonite Education" (1971)

Concern 13 (1966)

    Albert J. Meyer and Walter Klaassen, "Church and Mennonite Colleges"

    Joanne Zerger Janzen, "The Bethel Experience in Retrospect"

    Walter Klaassen, "Christian Life at Conrad Grebel College"

    Henry Rempel, "The Bluffton College Christian Fellowship"

    Steve Behrends, "Christian Communal Living on the Tabor Campus"

    [Unattributed] "Tabor Christian Fellowship Association"

    Glenn M. Lehman, "The Church on Eastern Mennonite College Campus"

    Harold E. Bauman, "The Church on Campus, Present and Future: What are the Issues?"

    Virgil Vogt, "Afterword"

APPENDIX: *CONCERN* REPUBLICATION VOLUMES

CONCERN *for the Church in the World: Essays on Christian Responsibility, 1958-1963*, ed. Laura Schmidt Roberts. Eugene, OR: Wipf & Stock, 2022.

Laura Schmidt Roberts, "Series Foreword"

Laura Schmidt Roberts, "Introduction"

Gordon D. Kaufman, "Nonresistance and Responsibility" (CONCERN 6, 1958)

Albert J. Meyer, "A Second Look at Responsibility" (CONCERN 6)

David Habegger, "Nonresistance and Responsibility —A Critical Analysis" (CONCERN 7, 1959)

John Howard Yoder, "The Otherness of the Church" (CONCERN 8, 1960)

CONCERN 10 (1961)

Jan M. Lochmann, "Christian Thought in the Age of the Cold War"

Albert Gaillard, "Christians and Marxists"

Katharina van Drimmelen, "Where Are the Firemen?"

John Howard Yoder, "The Christian Answer to Communism"

John Howard Yoder, "Marginalia"

CONCERN 11 (1963)

Karl Barth, "Poverty"

Andrew Murray, "The Poverty of Christ"

R. Mehl, "Money"

Virgil Vogt, "God or Mammon"

John Howard Yoder, "Marginalia"

Melissa Florer-Bixler, "All Economy Is Atheist: Towards a Non-Competitive Hope for the Church in the World"

Appendix: CONCERN republication volumes content list

APPENDIX: *CONCERN* REPUBLICATION VOLUMES

Concern *for Church Renewal: Essays on Community and Discipleship, 1958–1966*, ed. Laura Schmidt Roberts. Eugene, OR: Wipf & Stock, 2022.

Laura Schmidt Roberts, "Series Foreword"

Laura Schmidt Roberts, "Introduction"

John Howard Yoder, "Marginalia" excerpt (Concern 8, 1960)

John Howard Yoder, "Marginalia" excerpt (Concern 5, 1958)

Hans-Ruedi Weber, "The Church in the House" (Concern 5)

Quintus Leatherman, "The House Church in the New Testament" (Concern 5)

Paul M. Miller, "Can the Sunday School Class Be the 'House' within which the True Church Is Experienced?" (Concern 5)

Albert Steiner, "Group Dynamics in Evangelism [by Paul Miller]: A Review Article" (Concern 8)

Gerald C. Studer, "Evangelism Through the Dynamics of a Christian Group" (Concern 5)

Virgil Vogt, "Small Congregations" (Concern 5)

Concern 12 (1966)

Leland Harder, "Changing Forms of the Church and Her Witness"

John W. Miller, "The Renewal of the Church"

John Howard Yoder, "Marginalia: A Syllabus of Issues"

Lewis Benson, "The Order that Belongs to the Gospel" (Concern 7, 1959)

Susanne Guenther Loewen, "After Yoder: Failure, Authenticity, and the Renewal of the Mennonite Church"

César García, "A Global Communion as a Condition for the Possibility of Church Renewal"

Appendix: Concern republication volumes content list

APPENDIX: *CONCERN* REPUBLICATION VOLUMES

CONCERN *for Church Mission and Spiritual Gifts: Essays on Faith and Culture, 1958–1968*, ed. Laura Schmidt Roberts. Eugene, OR: Wipf & Stock, 2022.

Laura Schmidt Roberts, "Series Foreword"

Laura Schmidt Roberts, "Introduction"

Paul Peachey, "Churchless Christianity" (CONCERN 7, 1959)

M. H. Grumm, "The Search for Guaranteed Survival" (CONCERN 8, 1960)

Edmund Perry, "The Christian Mission to the Resurgent Religions" (CONCERN 9, 1961)

John Howard Yoder, "A Light to the Nations" (CONCERN 9)

Paul Peachey, "The End of Christendom" (CONCERN 9)

CONCERN 15 (1967)

John Howard Yoder, "Marginalia"

James Fairfield, "Tongues, a Testimony"

Herb Klassen and Maureen Klassen "You Shall Receive . . . "

S. Djojodihardjo, "An Experience in My Life"

Donald R. Jacobs, "The Charismatic in East Africa"

Myron S. Augsburger, "The Charismatic Aspects of the Work of the Spirit"

Irvin B. Horst, "A Historical Estimate of the Charismatic Movement"

Gerald C. Studer, "The Charismatic Revival: A Survey of the Literature"

Werner Schmauch, "The Prophetic Office in the Church" (CONCERN 5, 1958)

CONCERN 16 (1968)

Henderson Nylrod, "Nasty Noel"

William Roberts Miller, "Pious Jingle Bells and the Coming of Christ"

Marlin Jeschke, "Getting Christ Back Out of Christmas"

John Howard Yoder, "On the Meaning of Christmas"

APPENDIX: *CONCERN* REPUBLICATION VOLUMES

John Howard Yoder and Virgil Vogt, "Marginalia: The Case Against Christmas"

Hyung Jin Kim Sun, "Global Anabaptist Movement: From Cross-cultural to Multicultural to Intercultural"

Andrés Pacheco Lozano, "Mission and Margin(alization): An Ecumenically-Shaped Anabaptist/Mennonite Approach to Mission"

Appendix: CONCERN republication volumes content list

CONCERN *for Church Polity and Discipline: Essays on Pastoral Ministry and Communal Authority, 1958–1969*, ed. Laura Schmidt Roberts. Eugene, OR: Wipf & Stock, 2022.

Laura Schmidt Roberts, "Series Foreword"

Laura Schmidt Roberts, "Introduction"

Gerald C. Studer, "Second Thoughts on the Pastoral Ministry" (CONCERN 6, 1958)

[Unattributed] "Marginalia" excerpt (CONCERN 6)

A. H. A. Bakker, "Efficiency in the Church" (CONCERN 7, 1959)

Edgar Metzler, "The Need to Which We Minister" (CONCERN 7)

Lewis Benson, "The Church's One Foundation" (CONCERN 8, 1960)

Walter Klaassen, "The Preacher and Preaching" (CONCERN 9, 1961)

William Klassen, "Discipleship and Church Order: A Review and Discussion" (CONCERN 9)

Walter Klaassen, "New Presbyter Is Old Priest Write Large" (CONCERN 17, 1969)

J. Lawrence Burkholder, "Theological Education for the Believers' Church" (CONCERN 17)

Virgil Vogt, "Marginalia" excerpt (CONCERN 17)

Elmer Ediger, "*Studies in Church Discipline*: A Review Article" (CONCERN 5, 1958)

William Klassen, "Some Neglected Aspects in the Biblical View of the Church" (CONCERN 8)

Calvin Redekop, "Postulates Concerning Religious Intentional Ethnic Groups" (CONCERN 9)

Balthasar Hubmaier, "On Fraternal Admonition" (CONCERN 14, 1967)

Don Jacobs, "Walking Together in East Africa" (CONCERN 14)

Samuel Shoemaker, "Dealing with Other People's Sins" (CONCERN 14)

Kimberly Penner, "Toward Ecclesial Practices and Notions of Authority that Embody Radical Hope"

Isaac S. Villegas, "The Ecclesial Flesh of Anabaptist Visions"

Appendix: CONCERN republication volumes content list

CONCERN *for Anabaptist Renewal: A Radical Reformation Reader, 1971*, ed. Virgil Vogt and Laura Schmidt Roberts. Eugene, OR: Wipf & Stock, 2022.

Editor's Note

John Roth, "Foreword"

CONCERN 18 (1971)

Virgil Vogt, "Introduction"

John Howard Yoder, "The Recovery of the Anabaptist Vision"

Harold S. Bender, "The Mennonite Conception of the Church and Its Relation to Community Building"

Harold S. Bender, "The Anabaptist Theology of Discipleship"

William Klassen, "Anabaptist Studies"

Walter Klaassen, "Radical Reformation"

Harold S. Bender, "The Pacifism of the Sixteenth Century Anabaptists"

"Anabaptism: An Introductory Bibliography"

Appendix: CONCERN republication volumes content list

Bibliography

Barry, David W. "The Successful Inner-City Church." *The City Church* 10.5 (1959) 6–7, 15.
Bender, Harold S. "The Mennonite Conception of the Church and Its Relation to Present Day Needs." *The Mennonite Quarterly Review* 19.2 (1945) 90–100.
Bergen, Jeremy M. "Whether, and How, a Church Ought to Repent for a Historical Wrong." *Theology Today* 73.2 (2016) 129–48.
Berger, Peter. *The Noise of Solemn Assemblies: Christian Commitment and the Religious Establishment in America*. Garden City: Doubleday, 1961.
———. "Whence the Rugged Individualist?" *Renewal* 3.9 (December 1963) 8–9.
Berry, Malinda E. "Avoiding Avoidance: Why I Assigned *Body Politics* this Spring." *Mennonite Life* 68 (2014). https://mla.bethelks.edu/ml-archive/2014/avoiding-avoidance-why-i-assigned-body-politics-th.php.
———. "Yoderian Messianism Isn't My Cup of Tea." https://syndicate.network/symposia/theology/messianic-political-theology-and-diaspora-ethics/.
Brown, Robert McAfee. "Two Books by Berger: An Assembly of Solemn Noises." *Union Seminary Quarterly Review* 17.4 (1962) 333–43.
Bruce, Alexander Balmain. "ΤΟ ΚΑΤΑ ΜΑΤΘΑΙΟΝ ΑΓΙΟΝ ΕΥΑΓΓΕΛΙΟΝ." In *The Expositor's Greek New Testament*, edited by W. Robertson Nicoll, 1:61–340. Grand Rapids: Eerdmans, 1956.
Burkholder, J. Lawrence. "The Peace Churches as Communities of Discernment." *The Christian Century* 80.36 (1963) 1072–75.
Casteel, John L. "Introduction: The Rise of Personal Groups." In *Spiritual Renewal Through Personal Groups*, edited by John L. Casteel, 17–25. New York: Association, 1957.
Castro, Jennifer, ed. *I've Got the Power: Naming and Reclaiming Power as a Force for Good*. Elkhart: Women in Leadership Project, Mennonite Church USA, 2018.
Chapman, Audrey R. "Truth Commissions as Instruments of Forgiveness and Reconciliation." In *Forgiveness and Reconciliation: Religion, Public Policy, and Conflict Transformation*, edited by Raymond G. Helmick et al., 257–78. Philadelphia: Templeton Foundation, 2001.
"Confession of Faith in a Mennonite Perspective." https://www.weaverland.org/wp-content/uploads/2017/07/1995-Confession-of-Faith-in-a-Mennonite-Perspective.pdf.
Cosby, Gordon. "Not Renewal, but Reformation." *Renewal* 3.3 (April 1963) 4–5.

Cramer, David, et al. "Theology and Misconduct: The Case of John Howard Yoder." *The Christian Century*, August 20, 2014. https://www.christiancentury.org/article/2014-07/theology-and-misconduct.

"Deep in the Heart of Texas: Highland Park Methodist, Dallas-A Mighty Church in the Booming Southwest." *The Christian Century*, November 12, 1952, 1312–18.

Driver, John. "The Kingdom of God: Goal of Messianic Mission." In *The Transfiguration of Mission: Biblical, Theological, & Historical Foundations*, edited by Wilbert R. Shenk, 83–105. Scottdale: Herald, 1993.

Ferre, Nels F. S. "A Theology for Missions." *The Christian Century*, November 21, 1962, 1444–45.

Filson, Floyd. "The Significance of the Early House Churches." *Journal of Biblical Literature* 58.2 (1939) 105–12.

Fox, George. "George Fox's Epistles." MS Box Q4/5, microfilm 813. Library of the Society of Friends, Friends House, London.

———. Henry J. Cadbury papers. HC.MC.1121. Quaker & Special Collections, Haverford College, Haverford, PE. http://archives.tricolib.brynmawr.edu/repositories/5/resources/581.

———. *The Journals of George Fox*. 8th ed. 2 vols. London: London Friends' Tract Association, 1891.

———. *The Works of George Fox*. 8 vols. Philadelphia: Gould, 1831.

Fox, George, et al. *Annual Catalogue of George Fox's Papers, Compiled in 1694–1697*. Philadelphia: Friends Bookstore, 1939.

Greer, Scott A. *Social Organization*. New York: Random House, 1955.

Guenther Loewen, Susanne. "Can the Cross Be 'Good News' for Women? Mennonite Peace Theology and the Suffering of Women." *Anabaptist Witness* 3.2 (2016) 109–21.

Guth, Karen V. "Doing Justice to the Complex Legacy of John Howard Yoder: Restorative Justice Resources in Witness and Feminist Ethics." *Journal of the Society of Christian Ethics* 25.2 (2015) 119–39.

———. "Moral Injury, Feminist and Womanist Ethics, and Tainted Legacies." *Journal of the Society of Christian Ethics* 38.1 (2018) 167–86.

Hauerwas, Stanley, and William H. Willimon. *Resident Aliens: Life in the Christian Colony*. Nashville: Abingdon, 1989.

Hershberger, Guy F. *The Recovery of the Anabaptist Vision*. Scottdale: Herald, 1957.

Hershberger, Nathan. "Power, Tradition, and Renewal: The Concern Movement and the Fragmented Institutionalization of Mennonite Life." *Mennonite Quarterly Review* 87 (2013) 155–86.

Hopwood, Percy G. S. *The Religious Experience of the Primitive Church*. Edinburgh: T. & T. Clark, 1936.

Jones, Serene. *Trauma and Grace: Theology in a Ruptured World*. Louisville: Westminster John Knox, 2009.

Krall, Ruth. "Living Inside the Hurricane's Eye, Part Five." In *Living on the Edge of the Edge: Letters to a Younger Colleague*, by Ruth E. Krall and Lisa Schirch, 91–114. Victoria: Friesen, 2017.

———. "Tales from the Reptile House." In *Living on the Edge of the Edge: Letters to a Younger Colleague*, by Ruth E. Krall and Lisa Schirch, 139–58. Victoria: Friesen, 2017.

———. "The Writers Voice and Particularity." In *Living on the Edge of the Edge: Letters to a Younger Colleague*, by Ruth E. Krall and Lisa Schirch, 11–28. Victoria: Friesen, 2017.
Krehbiel, Stephanie. "Pacifist Battlegrounds: Violence, Community, and the Struggle for LGBTQ Justice in the Mennonite Church USA." PhD diss., University of Kansas, 2015.
Littell, Franklin H. *The Free Church*. Boston: Starr King, 1957.
Lloyd, Roger B. *An Adventure in Discipleship: The Servants of Christ the King*. New York: Longmans, Green, 1953.
Lohfink, Gerhard. *La Iglesia Que Jesús Quería: Dimensión Comunitaria de la Fe Cristiana*. 4a ed. Bilbao, Spain: Deslee de Brouwer, 1986.
Luccock, Halford E. "The Gospel According to St. Mark: Exposition." In *The Interpreter's Bible*, edited by George A. Buttrick et al, 7:647–917. New York: Abingdon-Cokesbury, 1951.
MacDonald, Alexander B. *Christian Worship in the Primitive Church*. Edinburgh: T. & T. Clark, 1934.
McClellan, Graydon. "The Ministry." In *New Frontiers of Christianity*, edited by Ralph C. Raughley Jr., 123–37. New York: Association, 1962.
Miller, Paul M. *Group Dynamics in Evangelism*. Scottdale: Herald, 1958.
Morton, Ralph T. "The House Church: Next Step or a First Step?" *The Coracle: The Journal of the Iona Community* 28 (March 1956) 1–8.
Neufeld Harder, Lydia. *The Challenge Is in the Naming: A Theological Journey*. Winnipeg: Canadian Mennonite University Press, 2018.
Newbigin, Lesslie. *The Household of God: Lectures on the Nature of the Church*. New York: Friendship, 1954.
O'Connor, Elizabeth. *Call to Commitment: The Story of the Church of the Saviour, Washington, D.C.* New York: Harper & Row, 1963.
Penner, Carol. "Content to Suffer: An Exploration of Mennonite Theology from the Context of Violence Against Women." In *Peace Theology and Violence against Women*, edited by Elizabeth G. Yoder, 99–111. Elkhart: Institute of Mennonite Studies, 1992.
———. "Mennonite Silences and Feminist Voices: Peace Theology and Violence against Women." PhD diss., University of St. Michael's College, 1999.
Plumptre, E. H. "The Gospel According to Matthew." In *A New Testament Commentary for English Readers*, edited by Charles John Ellicott, 1:1–186. 3 vols. 3rd ed. London: Cassell, Petter, & Galpin, 1877–79.
Robinson, John A. T. "The House Church." *Theology* 56.398 (1953) 303–5.
———. "The House Church and the Parish Church." *Theology* 53.362 (1950) 283–89.
Rose, Stephen C. "The Marks of Renewal." *Renewal* 3.9 (1963) 6–8.
———. "A Positive Program." *Renewal* 3.9 (1963) 10–13.
Sawatsky, Rodney. "Editorial." *The Conrad Grebel Review* 8.2 (1990) iii–iv.
Scarsella, Hilary Jerome. "Hope and the Work that Gets Us There: Insights for Communities Engaging Survivors." *Our Stories Untold* (blog), June 12, 2019. www.ourstoriesuntold.com/hope-and-the-work-that-gets-us-there/?fbclid=IwAR22ipTo D7hHeAFGPDKdxNCgPEU1dsR2WneKVpL84WEzwE23lP11O0_ZSM8.
———. "Not Making Sense: Why Stanley Hauerwas's Response to Yoder's Sexual Abuse Misses the Mark." *ABC Religion and Ethics*, November 30, 2017. https://www.abc.net.au/religion/not-making-sense-why-stanley-hauerwass-response-to-yoders-sexual/10095168.

Scarsella, Hilary Jerome, and Stephanie Krehbiel. "Sexual Violence: Christian Theological Legacies and Responsibilities." *Religion Compass* 13.9 (2019) e12337. https://doi.org/10.1111/rec3.12337.

Scarsella, Hilary Jerome, et al. "The Lord's Supper: A Ritual of Harm or Healing?" *Leader* (2016) 33–48.

Schirch, Lisa. "To the Next Generation of Pacifist Theologians." In *Living on the Edge of the Edge: Letters to a Younger Colleague*, by Ruth E. Krall and Lisa Schirch, 285–300. Victoria: Friesen, 2017.

Shippey, Frederick. *Church Work in the City*. New York: Abingdon-Cokesbury, 1952.

Snyder, Ross. "Members One of Another . . ." *International Journal of Religious Education* 33.9 (1957) 8–9.

Soto Albrecht, Elizabeth, and Darryl W. Stephens, eds. *Liberating the Politics of Jesus: Renewing Peace Theology through the Wisdom of Women*. London: T. & T. Clark, 2020.

Southcott, E. W. *The Parish Comes Alive*. New York: Morehouse-Gorham, 1956.

Stephenson, Dwight E. "Only Christ and Each Other." *International Journal of Religious Education* 33.9 (May 1957) 10–11.

Thornton, Lionel S. *The Common Life in the Body of Christ*. London: Dacre, 1942.

Toews, Paul. *Mennonites in American Society, 1930–1970: Modernity and the Persistence of Religious Community*. Scottdale: Herald, 1996.

Villegas, Isaac Samuel. "The Ecclesial Ethics of John Howard Yoder's Abuse." *Modern Theology* 37.1 (2021) 191–214. https://onlinelibrary.wiley.com/doi/epdf/10.1111/moth.12623.

Vogt, Virgil, ed. *CONCERN for Education: Essays on Christian Higher Education, 1958–1966*. Eugene, OR: Wipf & Stock, 2010.

———. *The Roots of CONCERN: Writings on Anabaptist Renewal, 1952–1957*. Eugene, OR: Wipf & Stock, 2009.

Vogt, Virgil, and Laura Schmidt Roberts, eds. *Concern for Anabaptist Renewal: A Radical Reformation Reader, 1971*. Eugene, OR: Wipf & Stock, 2022.

Wagoner, Walter D. *Bachelor of Divinity*. New York: Association, 1963.

Waltner Goossen, Rachel. "'Defanging the Beast': Mennonite Responses to John Howard Yoder's Sexual Abuse." *Mennonite Quarterly Review* 89.1 (2015) 7–80.

———. "Mennonite Bodies, Sexual Ethics: Women Challenge John Howard Yoder." *Journal of Mennonite Studies* 34 (2016) 247–59.

Weber, Hans-Ruedi. "The Church in the House." *Laity* 3 (1957) 37–57.

Wenger Shenk, Sara. "AMBS Response to Hilary Scarsella." https://www.ambs.edu/ambs-response-to-hilary-scarsella/.

———. "AMBS Response to Victims of John H. Yoder Abuse." https://www.ambs.edu/ambs-response-to-victims-of-john-howard-yoder-abuse/.

———. "Statement of Confession and Apology." https://ambs.edu/wp-content/uploads/2021/10/March22-Apology-and-Confession_SaraWengerShenk.pdf.

Williams, Colin. *Where in the World? Changing Forms of the Church's Witness*. New York: National Council of Churches, 1963.

Wink, Walter. *Engaging the Powers: Discernment and Resistance in a World of Domination*. Minneapolis: Fortress, 1992.

Winter, Gibson. *The New Creation as Metropolis*. New York: Macmillan, 1963.

———. *The Suburban Captivity of the Churches: An Analysis of Protestant Responsibility in the Expanding Metropolis*. New York: Macmillan, 1962.

Yoder, Elizabeth G., ed. *Peace Theology and Violence against Women*. Elkhart: Institute of Mennonite Studies, 1992.

Yoder, John Howard. *What Would You Do? A Serious Answer to a Standard Question*. Scottdale: Herald, 1983.

Younger, George D. "'Success' and 'Failure' in Inner-City Churches." In *Cities and Churches: Readings on the Urban Church*, edited by Robert Lee, 152–61. Philadelphia: Westminster, 1957.

www.ingramcontent.com/pod-product-compliance
Lightning Source LLC
Chambersburg PA
CBHW050811160426
43192CB00010B/1719